Floral QUILTS
FROM GRANDMA'S CUPBOARD

These thoroughly modern quilts hold little secrets straight from Grandma's cupboard. Can you guess what they are?

In each quilt, vintage feedsack scraps are stitched alongside reproduction fabrics. Finding those nostalgic patches is like touring a garden and discovering rare flowers that could only have been handed down through generations of gardeners. But anyone holding this book can own one or more of these very special quilts — all it takes is a selection of floral fabrics and a delight in creating beautiful things!

LEISURE ARTS, INC.
Little Rock, Arkansas

Meet the DESIGNER

Michelle Blackhurst's affection for flowers has blossomed into an extraordinary bouquet of quilts. However, Michelle didn't start her creative life as a quilter.

Needlepoint was Michelle's passion when she went to work at her local quilt shop a few years ago. When Michelle was asked to make an appliqué block for the shop's annual Christmas quilt, she balked.

"I didn't know a thing about appliqué," Michelle says. "I wasn't eager to learn it, either. Then one of my co-workers showed me how easy it is. That one block started it all. I was hooked!"

The eight original designs in this collection are the direct results of Michelle's conversion from needlepoint enthusiast to devoted quilter.

"Quilts are one of the good things in life," Michelle says. "Everyone should quilt."

Table of CONTENTS

Country PLEASURES

A house in the country, a garden of flowers, and lots of fresh honey for your tea. Could there possibly "bee" a better life? This little wall quilt with four Log Cabin blocks is a pleasant reminder that life isn't all work. Take time out to build your dream house ... it's as easy as relaxing with patchwork and appliqué.

COUNTRY PLEASURES

Finished Size: 59$\frac{1}{2}$" x 71$\frac{1}{2}$" (151 cm x 182 cm)

FABRIC REQUIREMENTS

$\frac{1}{2}$ yd (46 cm) of pink print for house background

$\frac{1}{2}$ yd (46 cm) of yellow print No. 1 for house background

$\frac{1}{2}$ yd (46 cm) of yellow print No. 2 for house background

$\frac{3}{4}$ yd (69 cm) of yellow print No. 3 for flower backgrounds

$\frac{3}{8}$ yd (34 cm) of yellow print No. 4 for side blocks

18" x 22" (46 cm x 56 cm) piece **each** of 4 assorted yellow prints for beehive backgrounds

$\frac{1}{2}$ yd (46 cm) **total** of assorted yellow prints

1 yd (91 cm) **total** of assorted green prints

$\frac{3}{8}$ yd (34 cm) **total** of assorted dark pink and red prints

$\frac{1}{4}$ yd (23 cm) **total** of assorted blue prints

$\frac{1}{4}$ yd (23 cm) **total** of assorted purple prints

$\frac{1}{2}$ yd (46 cm) of binding fabric

4 yds (3.6 m) of backing fabric

72" x 90" batting

CUTTING THE BACKGROUNDS, BLOCKS, AND BORDERS

*Yardage is based on 45"w fabric. Refer to **Rotary Cutting**, page 101, before beginning project.*

From pink print:
- Cut 1 house background rectangle (No. 1) 43" x 17$\frac{3}{4}$".

From yellow print No. 1:
- Cut 1 house background rectangle (No. 2) 22" x 17$\frac{3}{4}$".

From yellow print No. 2:
- Cut 1 house background rectangle (No. 3) 21$\frac{1}{2}$" x 17$\frac{3}{4}$".

From yellow print No. 3:
- Cut 2 flower background rectangles (No. 4) 24" x 18$\frac{1}{2}$".

From yellow print No. 4:
- Cut 2 side block rectangles (No. 5) 8$\frac{1}{2}$" x 19".

From assorted yellow prints:
- Cut 4 beehive background rectangles (No. 6) 18" x 18$\frac{1}{2}$".

From blue print:
- Cut 4 squares (No. 7) $2^1/_2$" x $2^1/_2$".

From assorted yellow prints:
- Cut 4 rectangles (No. 8) $1^1/_2$" x $2^1/_2$".
- Cut 4 rectangles (No. 9) $1^1/_2$" x $3^1/_2$".
- Cut 4 rectangles (No. 12) $1^1/_2$" x $4^1/_2$".
- Cut 4 rectangles (No. 13) $1^1/_2$" x $5^1/_2$".
- Cut 4 rectangles (No. 16) $1^1/_2$" x $6^1/_2$".
- Cut 4 rectangles (No. 17) $1^1/_2$" x $7^1/_2$".

From assorted dark pink and red prints:
- Cut 4 rectangles (No. 10) $1^1/_2$" x $3^1/_2$".
- Cut 4 rectangles (No. 11) $1^1/_2$" x $4^1/_2$".
- Cut 4 rectangles (No. 14) $1^1/_2$" x $5^1/_2$".
- Cut 4 rectangles (No. 15) $1^1/_2$" x $6^1/_2$".
- Cut 4 rectangles (No. 18) $1^1/_2$" x $7^1/_2$".
- Cut 4 rectangles (No. 19) $1^1/_2$" x $8^1/_2$".

From binding fabric:
- Cut 7 strips $2^1/_2$"w.

CUTTING THE APPLIQUÉS

Refer to **Making Templates**, *page 104, to use patterns, pages 10-19, to make templates.* **Note:** *Appliqué patterns provided do not include seam allowances. Measurements given for rectangles include* $1/_4$*"seam allowance. To help keep blocks organized, lay out all appliqué pieces with corresponding backgrounds as you cut.*

House Block

House

From assorted green prints:
- Cut 1 house side (A1 and A2).
- Cut 1 rectangle $9^1/_2$" x $10^1/_4$" for house front (B).
- Cut 1 door frame on fold (D).

From yellow print:
- Cut 1 roof (F1 and F2).

From assorted dark pink and red prints:
- Cut 1 rectangle $2^3/_4$" x $4^1/_4$" for door (C).
- Cut 1 rectangle 2" x $2^1/_2$" for chimney (E).
- Cut 1 side roof (G).
- Cut 3 (2 front and 1 side) window sashes (H).
- Cut 2 front window sashes (I).
- Cut 1 side window sash (J).
- Cut 2 front window frames on fold (K).
- Cut 1 side window frame on fold (L).

Left Flower

From assorted green prints:
- Cut 1 each of stems (M and N).
- Cut 1 stem (O1, O2, and O3).
- Cut 1 each of flower caps (S, W, and Y).
- Cut 1 each of leaves (Z, AA, and BB).

From purple print:
- Cut 1 flower (P).

From assorted dark pink and red prints:
- Cut 1 each of flowers (T and X).
- Cut 1 flower petal (U).
- Cut 1 each of flower centers (R and V).

From blue print:
- Cut 1 flower petal (Q).

Right Flower

From assorted green prints:
- Cut 1 each of stems (CC, DD, EE, and FF).
- Cut 1 stem (GG1, GG2, and GG3).
- Cut 1 each of flower caps (KK, MM, and QQ).
- Cut 8 leaves (RR).

From purple print:
- Cut 1 flower (NN).

From assorted dark pink and red prints:
- Cut 1 each of flowers (HH and LL).
- Cut 1 flower petal (II).
- Cut 1 each of flower centers (JJ and PP).

From blue print:
- Cut 1 flower petal (OO).

Beehive Block

From assorted yellow prints:
- Cut 2 beehive stripes; cut 2 in reverse for each piece (SS, TT, UU, and VV).
- Cut 2 beehives; cut 2 in reverse (WW).

From assorted red prints:
- Cut 4 beehive openings (XX).

From assorted dark pink, red, yellow, and blue prints:
- Cut 4 each of flowers (ZZ, b, d, and f).
- Cut 4 each of flower centers (a, c, e, and g).

From assorted green prints:
- Cut 2 stems; cut 2 in reverse (YY1 and YY2).
- Cut 2 leaves; cut 2 in reverse (h).
- Cut 2 leaves; cut 2 in reverse (i).
- Cut 2 leaves; cut 2 in reverse (j).

Flower Block

From assorted dark pink and red prints:
- Cut 8 flower petals on fold (k).
- Cut 2 flowers on fold (l).
- Cut 8 flower centers (m).

MAKING THE BLOCKS

*Refer to **Piecing and Pressing,** page 103, and **Needle-Turn Appliqué,** page 104, to assemble the blocks.*

House Block

Refer to **House Block Diagram** and **Quilt Top Diagram** for placement to sew the Nos. 1, 2, and 3 house background rectangles together to make quilt top center (**Unit 1**). Working in alphabetical order, position pieces, then pin or baste in place on **Unit 1**; appliqué.

House Block Diagram

Beehive Block

Refer to **Beehive Block Diagram** and **Quilt Top Diagram** for placement to make 4 blocks (2 in reverse). Working in alphabetical order, position pieces, then pin or baste in place on a No. 6 background block; appliqué.

Beehive Block Diagram

Flower Block

Refer to **Flower Block Diagram** and **Quilt Top Diagram** for placement to make 2 blocks. Working in alphabetical order, position pieces, then pin or baste in place on a No. 4 background block; appliqué.

Flower Block Diagram

Log Cabin Block

Refer to **Block Assembly Diagram** to piece the square and strips together in the order shown. Make 4 blocks.

Block Assembly Diagram

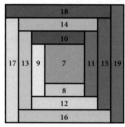

ASSEMBLING THE QUILT TOP

*Referring to the photo, page 6, and **Quilt Top Diagram** for placement, sew the blocks together in the order listed below.*

1. Sew 1 **Log Cabin Block** to the top and bottom of each No. 5 side block rectangle to make **Unit 2** and **Unit 3**.
2. Sew **Unit 2** and **Unit 3** to **Unit 1** to make **Unit 4**.
3. Sew 1 **Beehive Block** and 1 reverse **Beehive Block** to each **Flower Block** to make **Unit 5** and **Unit 6**.
4. Sew **Unit 5** and **Unit 6** to **Unit 4** to make quilt top.

FINISHING

1. Follow **Quilting**, page 106, to mark, layer, and quilt as desired. Our quilt was machine quilted.
2. Follow **Making Straight Grain Binding**, page 110, to make $7^5/8$ yds of $2^1/2$"w binding.
3. Follow **Attaching Binding with Mitered Corners**, page 110, to attach binding to quilt.

House Block

NOTE: For patterns with multiple pieces (e.g. pattern pieces labeled A1 and A2), match dashed lines and arrows to trace a complete pattern. For patterns marked with a dashed fold line, match fold of pattern to fold of fabric and cut out on solid lines.

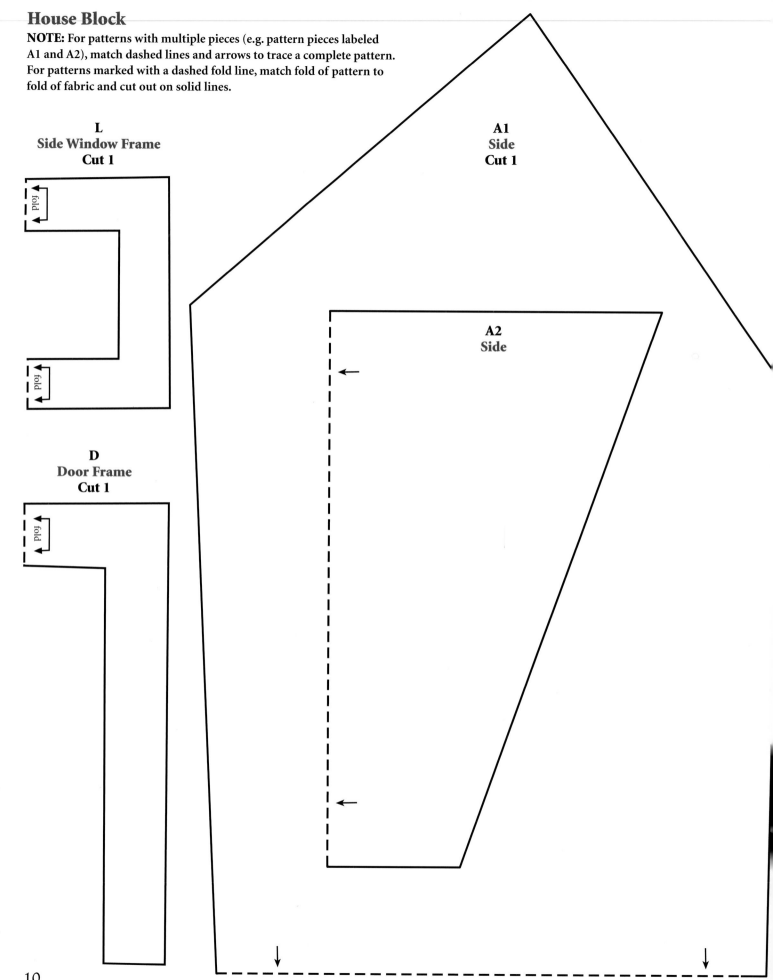

L
Side Window Frame
Cut 1

fold

fold

A1
Side
Cut 1

A2
Side

D
Door Frame
Cut 1

fold

10

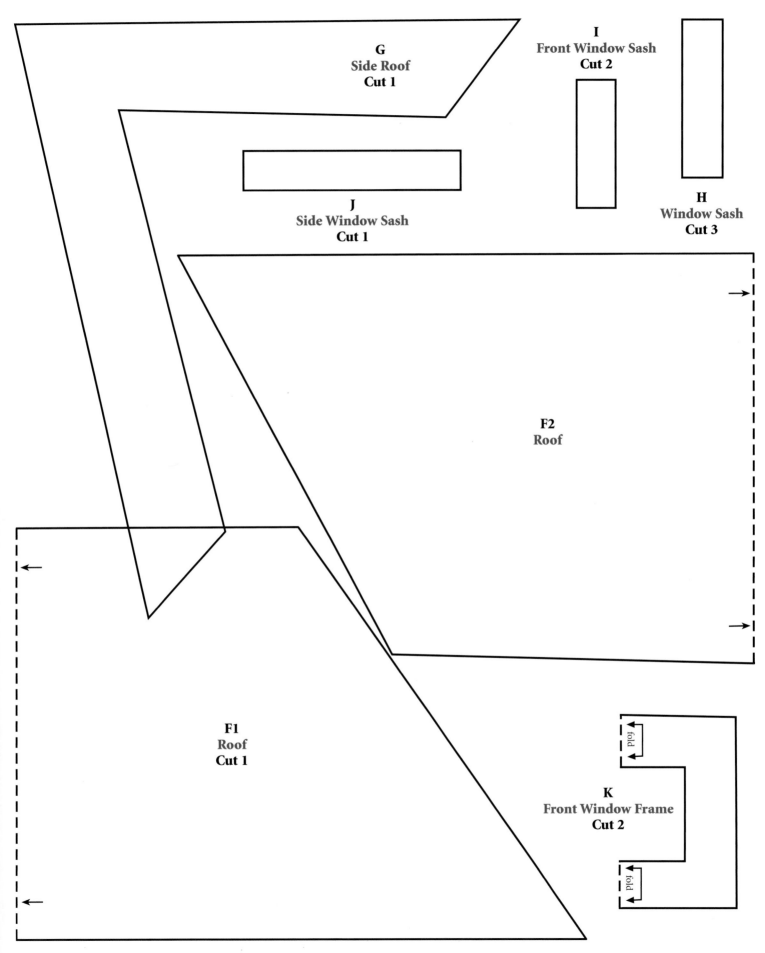

G
Side Roof
Cut 1

I
Front Window Sash
Cut 2

J
Side Window Sash
Cut 1

H
Window Sash
Cut 3

F2
Roof

F1
Roof
Cut 1

K
Front Window Frame
Cut 2

fold

fold

11

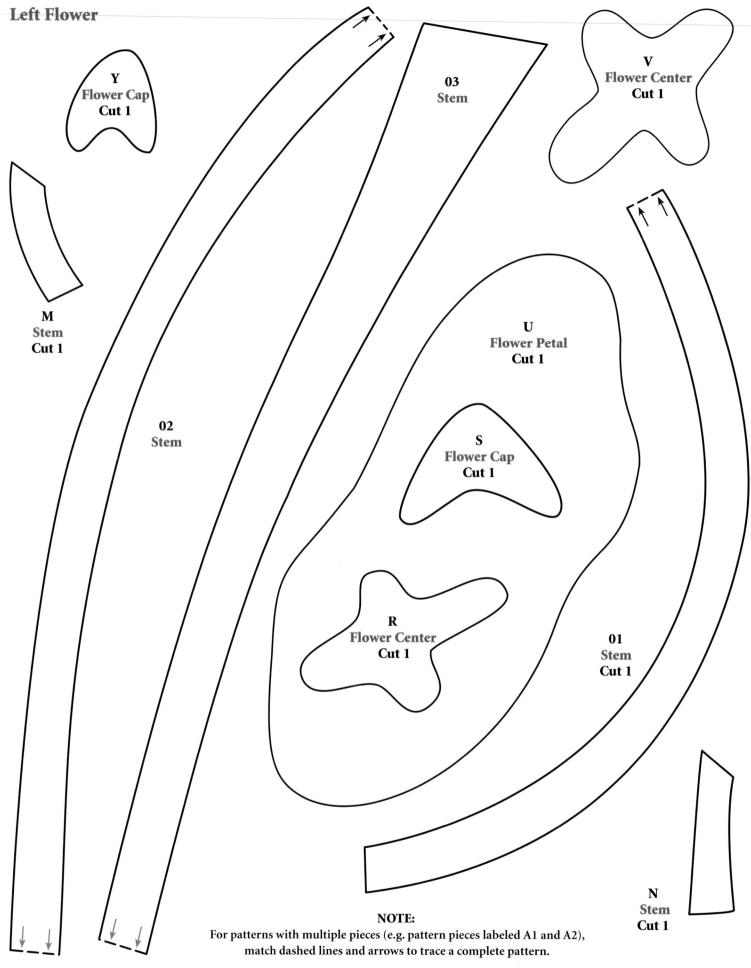

Left Flower

Y
Flower Cap
Cut 1

03
Stem

V
Flower Center
Cut 1

M
Stem
Cut 1

U
Flower Petal
Cut 1

02
Stem

S
Flower Cap
Cut 1

R
Flower Center
Cut 1

01
Stem
Cut 1

N
Stem
Cut 1

NOTE:
For patterns with multiple pieces (e.g. pattern pieces labeled A1 and A2),
match dashed lines and arrows to trace a complete pattern.

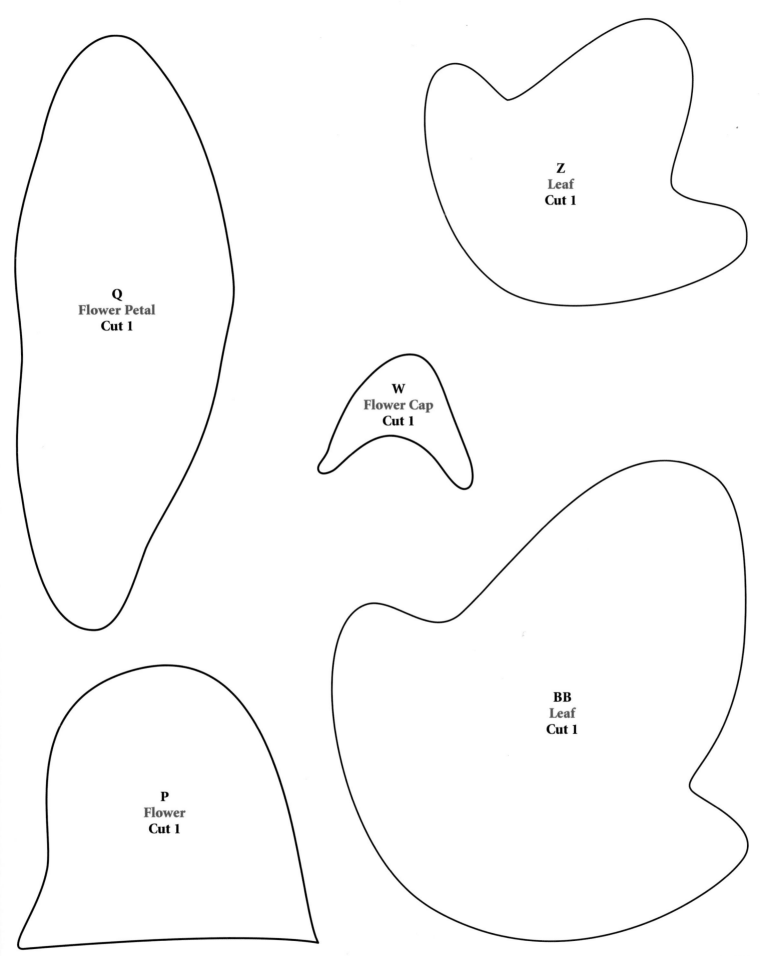

Q
Flower Petal
Cut 1

Z
Leaf
Cut 1

W
Flower Cap
Cut 1

BB
Leaf
Cut 1

P
Flower
Cut 1

13

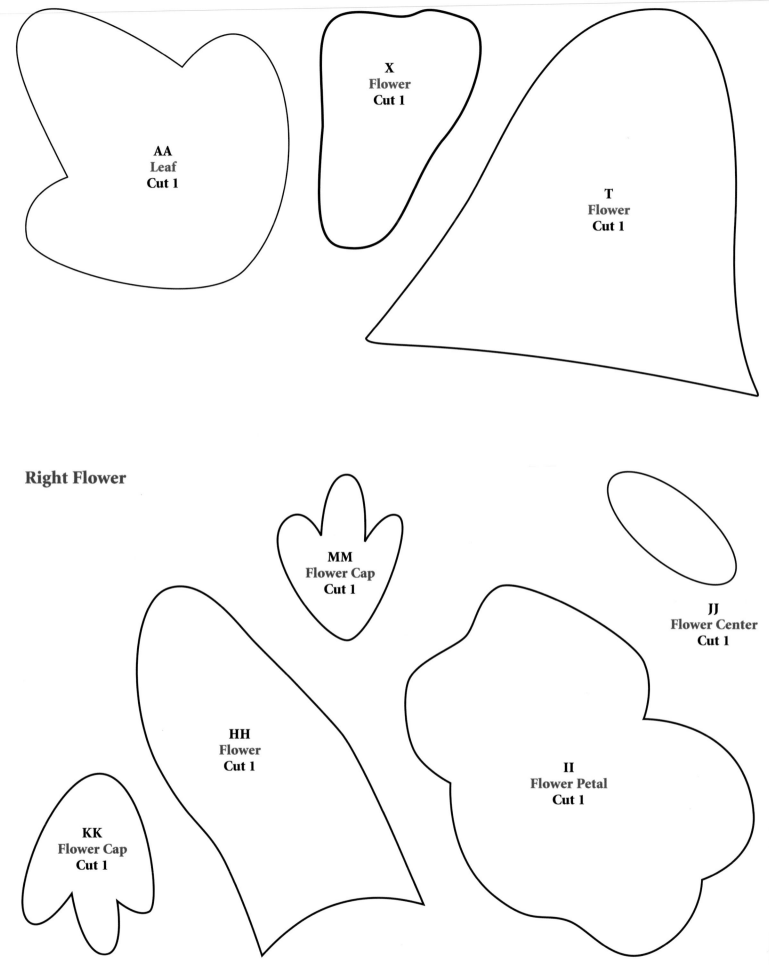

AA
Leaf
Cut 1

X
Flower
Cut 1

T
Flower
Cut 1

Right Flower

MM
Flower Cap
Cut 1

JJ
Flower Center
Cut 1

HH
Flower
Cut 1

II
Flower Petal
Cut 1

KK
Flower Cap
Cut 1

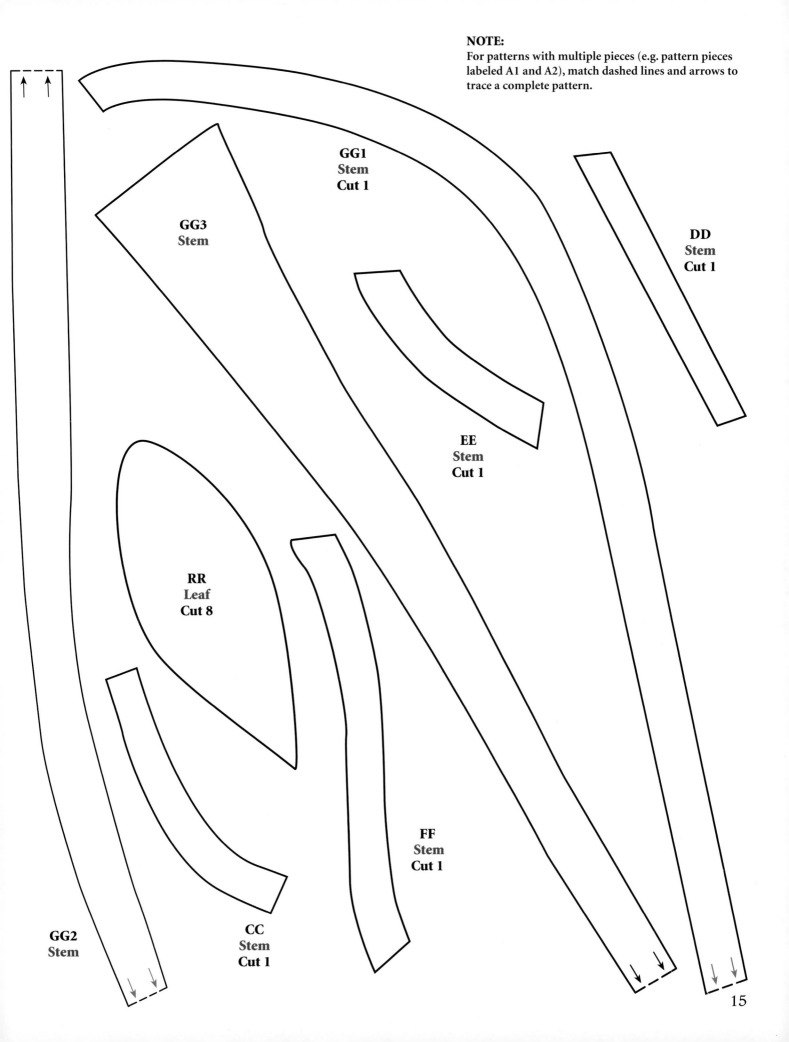

NOTE:
For patterns with multiple pieces (e.g. pattern pieces labeled A1 and A2), match dashed lines and arrows to trace a complete pattern.

GG1
Stem
Cut 1

GG3
Stem

DD
Stem
Cut 1

EE
Stem
Cut 1

RR
Leaf
Cut 8

FF
Stem
Cut 1

GG2
Stem

CC
Stem
Cut 1

15

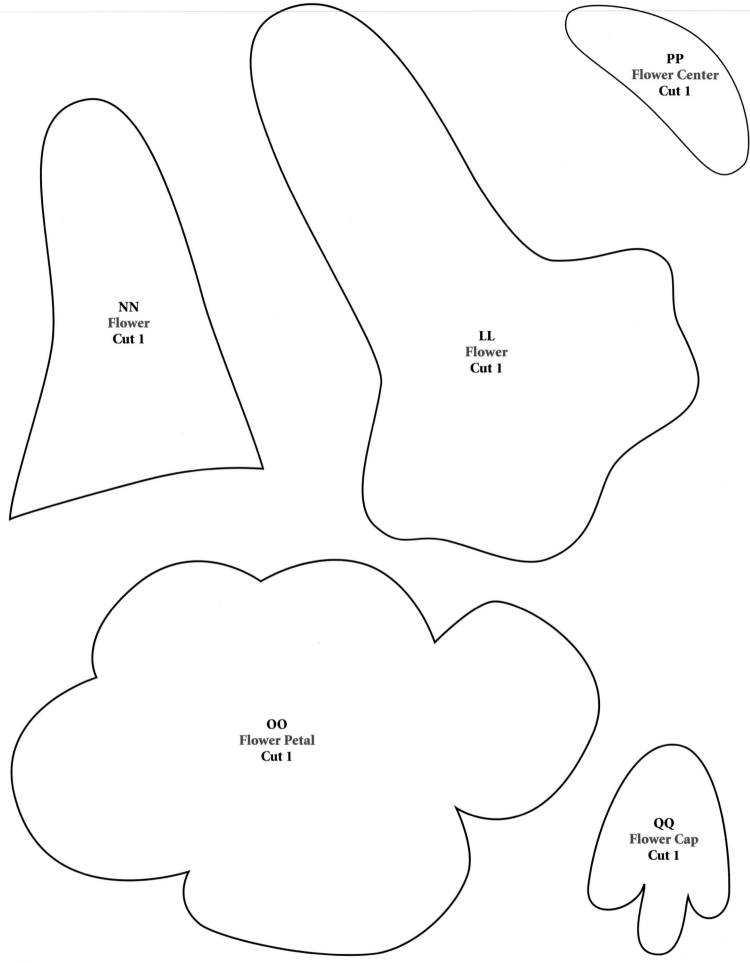

PP
Flower Center
Cut 1

NN
Flower
Cut 1

LL
Flower
Cut 1

OO
Flower Petal
Cut 1

QQ
Flower Cap
Cut 1

Beehive Block

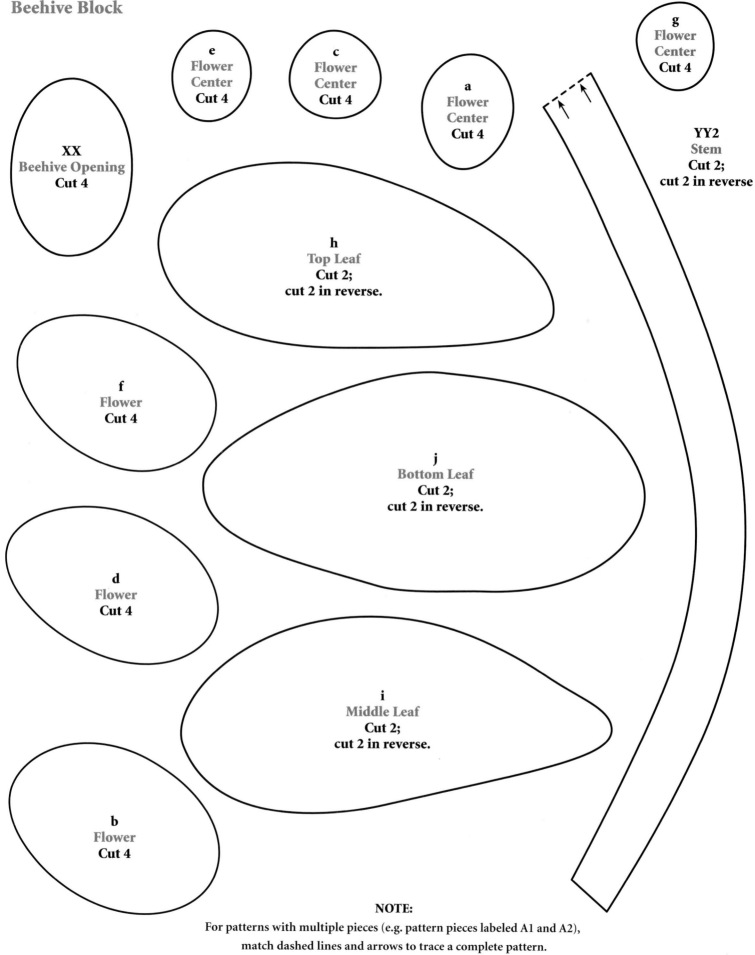

e
Flower
Center
Cut 4

c
Flower
Center
Cut 4

a
Flower
Center
Cut 4

g
Flower
Center
Cut 4

XX
Beehive Opening
Cut 4

YY2
Stem
Cut 2;
cut 2 in reverse

h
Top Leaf
Cut 2;
cut 2 in reverse.

f
Flower
Cut 4

j
Bottom Leaf
Cut 2;
cut 2 in reverse.

d
Flower
Cut 4

i
Middle Leaf
Cut 2;
cut 2 in reverse.

b
Flower
Cut 4

NOTE:
For patterns with multiple pieces (e.g. pattern pieces labeled A1 and A2),
match dashed lines and arrows to trace a complete pattern.

17

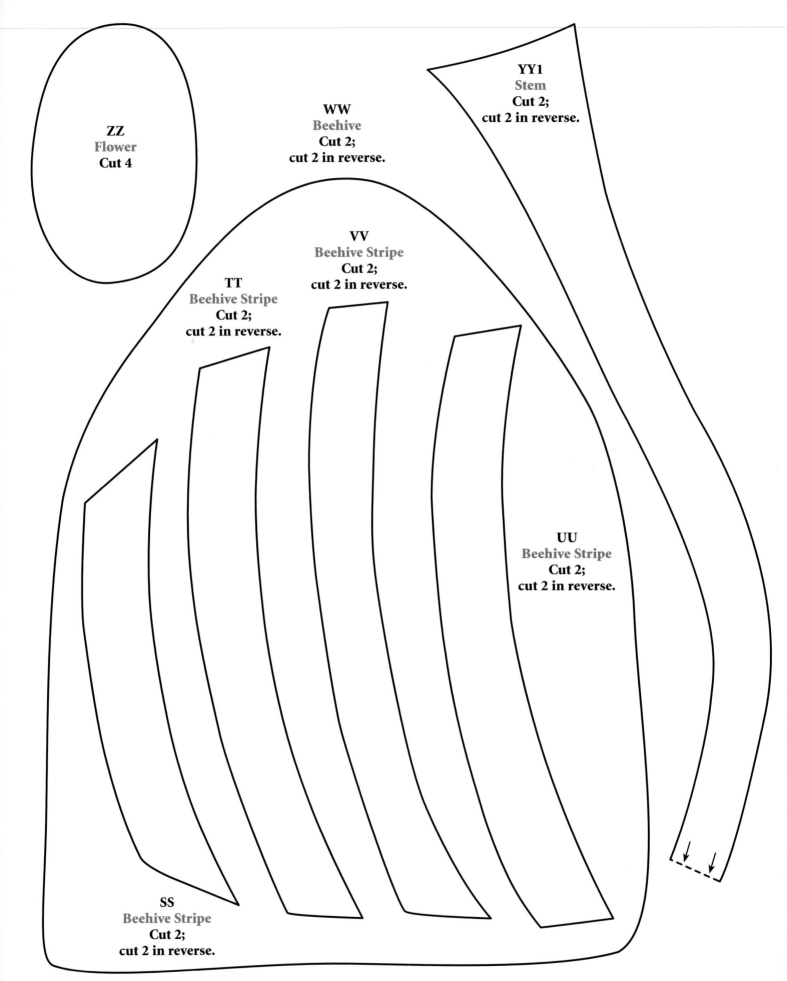

ZZ
Flower
Cut 4

WW
Beehive
Cut 2;
cut 2 in reverse.

YY1
Stem
Cut 2;
cut 2 in reverse.

VV
Beehive Stripe
Cut 2;
cut 2 in reverse.

TT
Beehive Stripe
Cut 2;
cut 2 in reverse.

UU
Beehive Stripe
Cut 2;
cut 2 in reverse.

SS
Beehive Stripe
Cut 2;
cut 2 in reverse.

Flower Block

NOTE: For patterns marked with a dashed fold line, match fold of pattern to fold of fabric and cut out on solid lines.

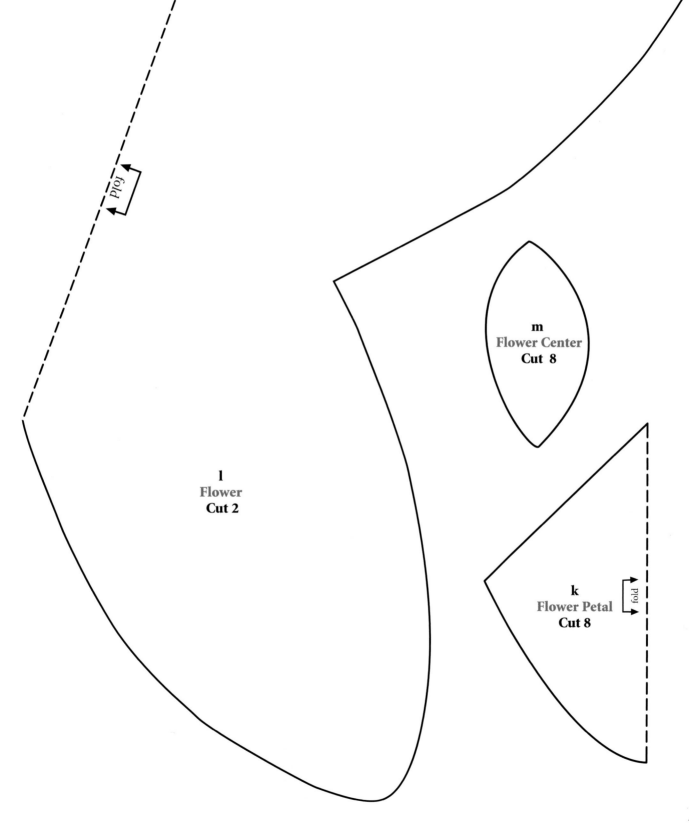

fold

m
Flower Center
Cut 8

l
Flower
Cut 2

k
Flower Petal
Cut 8

fold

Emmy's
FAVORITE

Blooming with foxgloves and buzzing with bees, Emmy's Favorite is sure to please — everyone! Michelle Blackhurst named this multi-flora quilt in honor of her feline friend, Emmy. It seems that most quilters have a cat ... or is it that most cats have a quilter?

EMMY'S FAVORITE
Finished Size: 69" x 77¹/₂" (175 cm x 197 cm)

FABRIC REQUIREMENTS

¹/₂ yd (46 cm) of yellow print No. 1
¹/₂ yd (46 cm) of yellow print No. 2
⁵/₈ yd (57 cm) of yellow print No. 3
¹/₂ yd (46 cm) of yellow print No. 4 for border
¹/₄ yd (23 cm) of yellow check for beehive
⁵/₈ yd (57 cm) of yellow plaid
¹/₂ yd (46 cm) of white print No. 1
⁵/₈ yd (57 cm) of white print No. 2
⁵/₈ yd (57 cm) of white print No. 3
¹/₂ yd (46 cm) of white print No. 4
¹/₂ yd (46 cm) of pink print No. 1
2 yds (1.8 m) of pink plaid for sashing
¹/₂ yd (46 cm) of pink print No. 2 for border

¹/₂ yd (46 cm) of blue stripe for border
¹/₂ yd (46 cm) of blue print for border
¹/₂ yd (46 cm) **total** of assorted green prints
¹/₄ yd (23 cm) **total** of assorted yellow prints
¹/₄ yd (23 cm) **total** of assorted pink prints
¹/₄ yd (23 cm) **total** of assorted blue prints
¹/₄ yd (23 cm) **total** of assorted purple prints
¹/₄ yd (23 cm) **total** of assorted red prints
⁵/₈ yd (57 cm) **total** of assorted pink fabrics for
    binding
4¹/₂ yds (4.1 m) of backing fabric
72" x 90" batting
Green embroidery floss

CUTTING THE BACKGROUNDS AND BORDERS

*Yardage is based on 45"w fabric. Refer to **Rotary Cutting**, page 101, before beginning project. To help keep pieces organized, refer to photo, page 22, to lay out the pieces as you cut.*

From yellow print No. 1:
- Cut 1 background rectangle (No. 1) 38" x 12".

From white print No. 2:
- Cut 1 background rectangle (No. 2) 18" x 16".

From white print No. 3:
- Cut 1 background rectangle (No. 3) 18" x 30".

From yellow plaid:
- Cut 1 background rectangle (No. 4) 19" x 24".

From yellow print No. 3:
- Cut 1 background rectangle (No. 5) 19" x 22".

From pink print No. 1:
- Cut 1 background rectangle (No. 6) $12^1/2$" x 13".

From white print No. 1:
- Cut 1 background rectangle (No. 7) $12^1/2$" x 13".

From yellow print No. 2:
- Cut 1 background rectangle (No. 8) $12^1/2$" x 13".

From white print No. 4:
- Cut 1 background rectangle (No. 9) $12^1/2$" x 18".

From pink plaid:
- Cut 1 sashing strip (No. 10) 38" x 2".
- Cut 1 sashing strip (No. 11) 18" x 2".
- Cut 1 sashing strip (No. 12) 19" x 2".
- Cut 3 sashing strips (Nos. 13, 14, and 15) $12^1/2$" x 2".
- Cut 1 sashing strip (No. 16) 2" x 47".
- Cut 1 sashing strip (No. 17) 2" x 60".
- Cut 2 sashing strips (Nos. 18 and 19) $51^1/2$" x 2".
- Cut 2 sashing strips (Nos. 20 and 21) 2" x 63".

From blue stripe:
- Cut 1 outer border (No. 22) $27^1/2$" x $7^1/2$".
- Cut 1 outer border (No. 23) $7^1/2$" x $39^1/2$".

From yellow print No. 4:
- Cut 1 outer border (No. 24) $7^1/2$" x 38".
- Cut 1 outer border (No. 25) $27^1/2$" x $7^1/2$".

From blue print:
- Cut 1 outer border (No. 26) $27^1/2$" x $7^1/2$".
- Cut 1 outer border (No. 27) $7^1/2$" x $39^1/2$".

From pink print No. 2:
- Cut 1 outer border (No. 28) $7^1/2$" x 38".
- Cut 1 outer border (No. 29) $27^1/2$" x $7^1/2$".

From assorted pink binding fabrics:
- Cut 7 strips $2^1/2$"w.

CUTTING THE APPLIQUÉS

*Refer to **Making Templates**, page 104, to use patterns, pages 28-35, to make templates. **Note:** Appliqué patterns provided do not include seam allowances. Measurements given for bias strips include a $1/4$" seam allowance. To help keep blocks organized, lay out all appliqué pieces with corresponding backgrounds as you cut.*

Block A

From assorted green prints:
- Cut 4 stems (A).
- Cut 8 leaves (B).

From assorted pink, blue, and purple prints:
- Cut 1 flower (C).
- Cut 1 flower (D).
- Cut 2 flowers (E).
- Cut 4 flower centers (F).

Blocks B1, B2, and B3

From assorted green prints:
- Cut 3 stems (G).
- Cut 6 leaves (H).
- Cut 1 flower part (K).

From assorted blue, yellow, red, and pink prints:
- Cut 3 flower bases (I).
- Cut 3 flower tops (J).
- Cut 2 flower parts (K).

Block C

From assorted green prints:
- Cut 1 each of stems (L, M, and N).
- Cut 3 leaves (O).

From assorted blue, pink, yellow, and purple prints:
- Cut 1 each of flowers (P, Q, and R).
- Cut 1 each of flower centers (S, T, and U).

Block D

From assorted green prints:
- Cut 1 each of stems (V, W, and X).
- Cut 9 leaves (Y).

From assorted pink prints:
- Cut 1 flower base (Z).
- Cut 4 side flower petals (AA).
- Cut 2 middle flower petals (BB).

From assorted yellow prints:
- Cut 2 flower bases (Z).
- Cut 2 side flower petals (AA).
- Cut 1 middle flower petal (BB).
- Cut 1 inner basket (DD).
- Cut 1 handle (EE).

From blue print:
- Cut 1 basket (CC).

Block E

From assorted green prints:
- Cut 3 bias strips (1" x 16^1/$_2$", 1" x 21", and 1" x 27") for stems.
- Cut 2 leaves (FF).
- Cut 1 leaf (GG).
- Cut 2 leaves (HH).
- Cut 1 leaf (II).
- Cut 2 leaves; cut 1 in reverse (JJ).
- Cut 9 circles (KK).

From assorted yellow, pink, and purple prints:
- Cut 7 flowers (LL).
- Cut 7 flower centers (MM).
- Cut 19 flowers (NN).
- Cut 19 flower centers (OO).

Block F

From yellow check:
- Cut 1 beehive on fold (PP).

From assorted blue prints:
- Cut 1 beehive opening (QQ).
- Cut 3 flower centers (VV).

From assorted green prints:
- Cut 3 stems (RR).
- Cut 18 leaves (SS).

From assorted pink and purple prints:
- Cut 3 flowers (TT).
- Cut 3 flower centers (UU).

Block G

From assorted green prints:
- Cut 1 stem (WW).
- Cut 3 leaves (XX).

From assorted pink prints:
- Cut 1 flower petal (YY).
- Cut 1 flower base (ZZ).
- Cut 1 flowerpot top (aa).

From blue print:
- Cut 1 flowerpot bottom (bb).

MAKING THE BLOCKS AND UNITS

*Refer to **Needle-Turn Appliqué**, page 104, for technique and **Piecing and Pressing,** page 103, to assemble the blocks. Refer to **Block Diagrams** and photo, page 22, for placement. Working in alphabetical order, position pieces, then pin or baste in place on a background rectangle before appliquéing.*

Unit 1

1. Appliqué stems, leaves, and flower pieces on a No. 1 background rectangle to make **Block A**.
2. Sew a No. 10 sashing strip to the bottom of the block to make **Unit 1**.

Unit 1

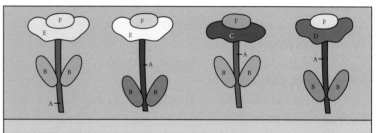

Units 2, 3, and 4

1. Appliqué stems, leaves, and flower pieces on Nos. 6, 7, and 8 background rectangles. Add stems with Stem Stitch using 3 strands of green embroidery floss to make **Blocks B1**, **B2**, and **B3**.
2. Sew a sashing strip (Nos. 13, 14, and 15) to the bottom of each block to make **Unit 2**, **Unit 3**, and **Unit 4**.

Units 2, 3, and 4

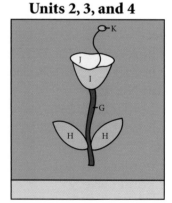

24

Unit 5

1. Appliqué stems, leaves, and flower pieces on the No. 2 background rectangle to make **Block C**.
2. Sew a No. 11 sashing strip to the bottom of the block to make **Unit 5**.

Unit 5

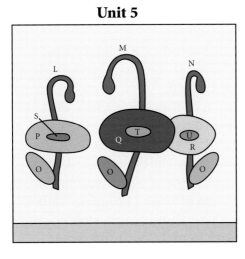

Unit 6

1. Appliqué stems, leaves, flower pieces, and basket pieces on the No. 4 background rectangle to make **Block D**.
2. Sew a No. 12 sashing strip to the bottom of the block to make **Unit 6**.

Unit 6

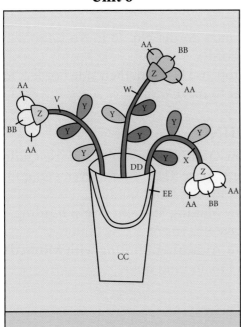

Block E

Appliqué stems, leaves, and flower pieces on the No. 3 background rectangle to make **Block E**.

Block E Diagram

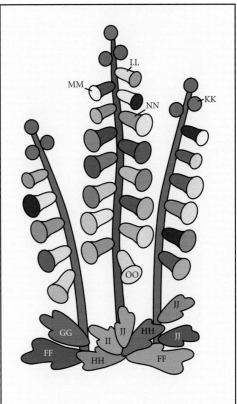

Block F

Appliqué stems, leaves, flower pieces, and beehive pieces on the No. 5 background rectangle to make **Block F**.

Block F Diagram

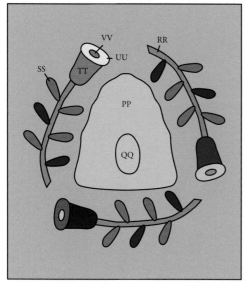

Block G

Appliqué stems, leaves, flower pieces, and flowerpot pieces on the No. 9 background rectangle to make **Block G**.

Block G Diagram

ASSEMBLING THE QUILT TOP

*Referring to **Quilt Top Diagram** and photo, page 22, for placement, sew the blocks together in the order listed below.*

1. Sew **Unit 2**, **Unit 3**, **Unit 4**, and **Block G** together to make **Unit 7**.
2. Sew a No. 17 sashing strip to the left side of **Unit 7** to make **Unit 8**.
3. Sew **Unit 5** to **Block E** to make **Unit 9**.
4. Sew a No. 16 sashing strip to the right side of **Unit 9** to make **Unit 10**.
5. Sew **Unit 6** to **Block F** to make **Unit 11**.
6. Sew **Unit 10** to **Unit 11** to make **Unit 12**.
7. Sew **Unit 1** to **Unit 12** to make **Unit 13**.
8. Sew **Unit 13** to **Unit 8** to make **Unit 14**.
9. Sew the No. 18 and No. 19 sashing strips to the top and bottom of **Unit 14** to make **Unit 15**.
10. Sew the No. 20 and No. 21 sashing strips to the sides of **Unit 15** to make quilt top center.

ADDING THE BORDERS

*Refer to **Quilt Top Diagram** and photo, page 22, for placement.*

1. Sew outer border No. 22 to No. 29 to make top border.
2. Sew outer border No. 25 to No. 26 to make bottom border.
3. Sew outer border No. 27 to No. 28 to make left side border.
4. Sew outer border No. 23 to No. 24 to make right side border.
5. Sew top and bottom, then side borders to quilt top center to make quilt.

FINISHING

1. Follow **Quilting**, page 106, and use **Quilting Pattern**, page 31, to mark, layer, and quilt as desired. Our quilt was hand quilted.
2. Follow **Making Straight Grain Binding**, page 110, to make 8$^3/_8$ yds of 2$^1/_2$"w binding.
3. Follow **Attaching Binding with Mitered Corners**, page 110, to bind quilt.

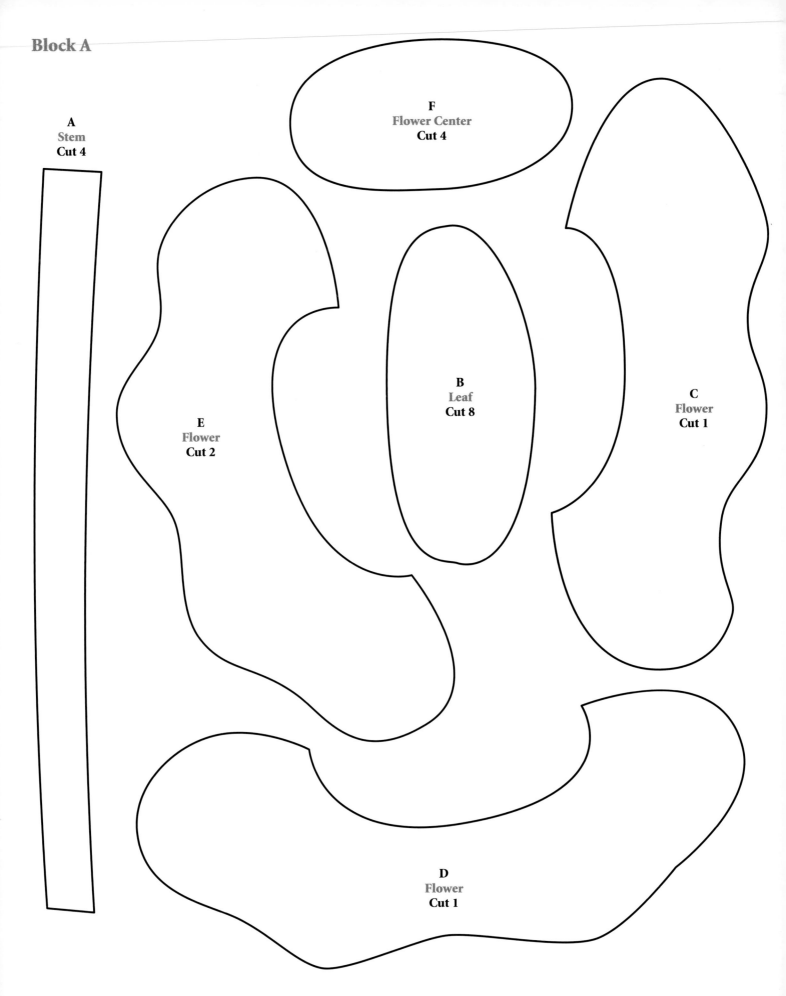

A
Stem
Cut 4

F
Flower Center
Cut 4

E
Flower
Cut 2

B
Leaf
Cut 8

C
Flower
Cut 1

D
Flower
Cut 1

Block B1, B2, and B3

Block C

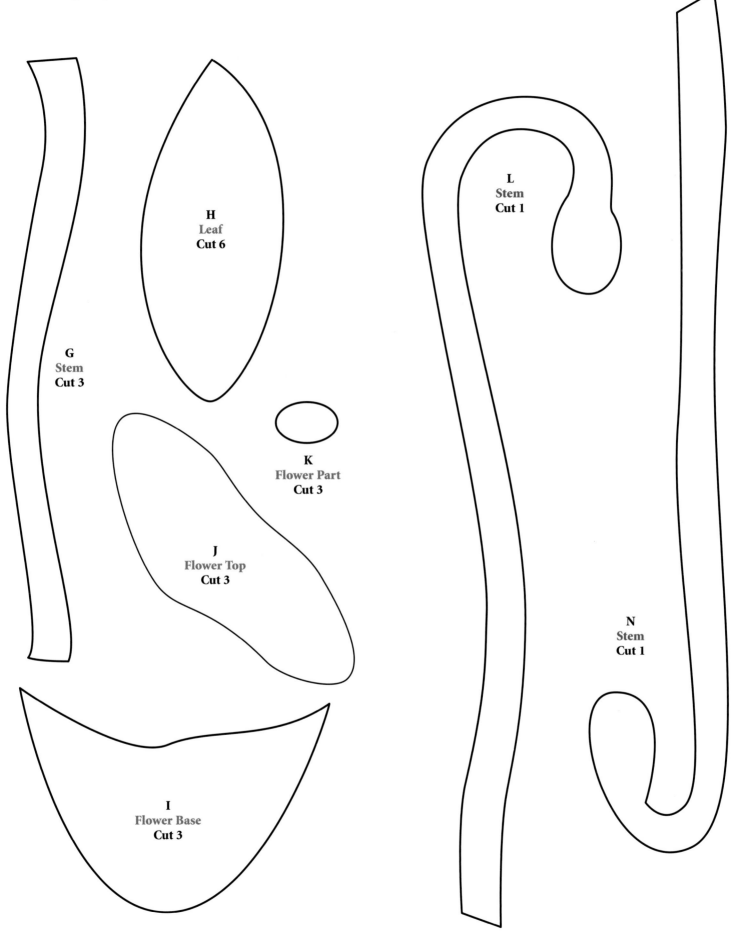

G
Stem
Cut 3

H
Leaf
Cut 6

K
Flower Part
Cut 3

J
Flower Top
Cut 3

I
Flower Base
Cut 3

L
Stem
Cut 1

N
Stem
Cut 1

29

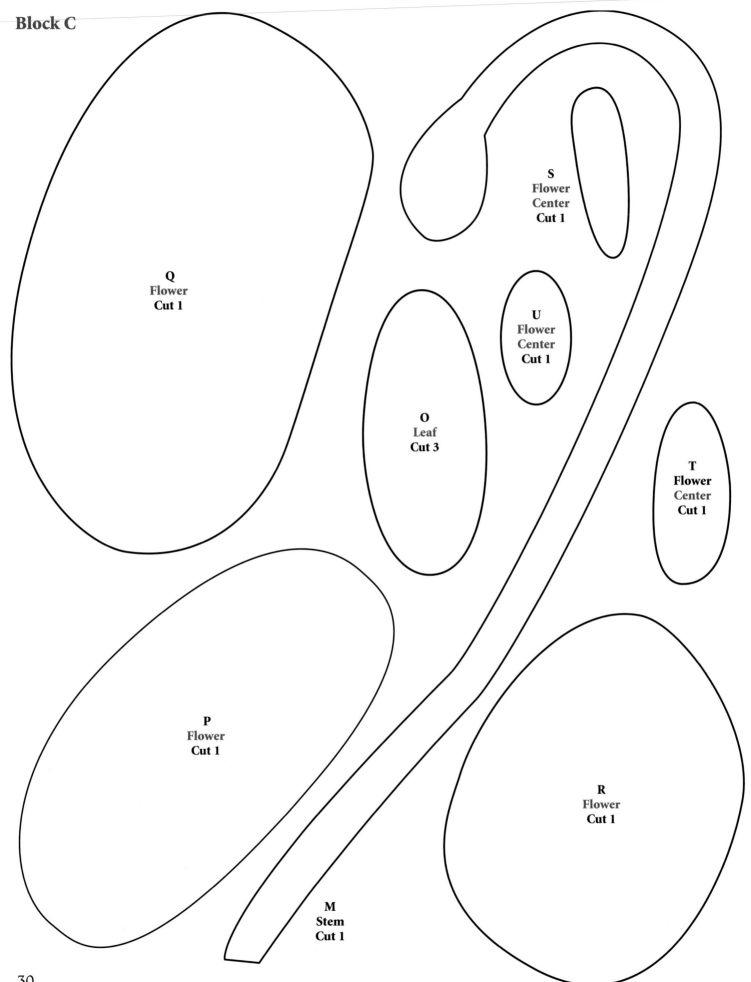

Q
Flower
Cut 1

S
Flower
Center
Cut 1

U
Flower
Center
Cut 1

O
Leaf
Cut 3

T
Flower
Center
Cut 1

P
Flower
Cut 1

R
Flower
Cut 1

M
Stem
Cut 1

Block D

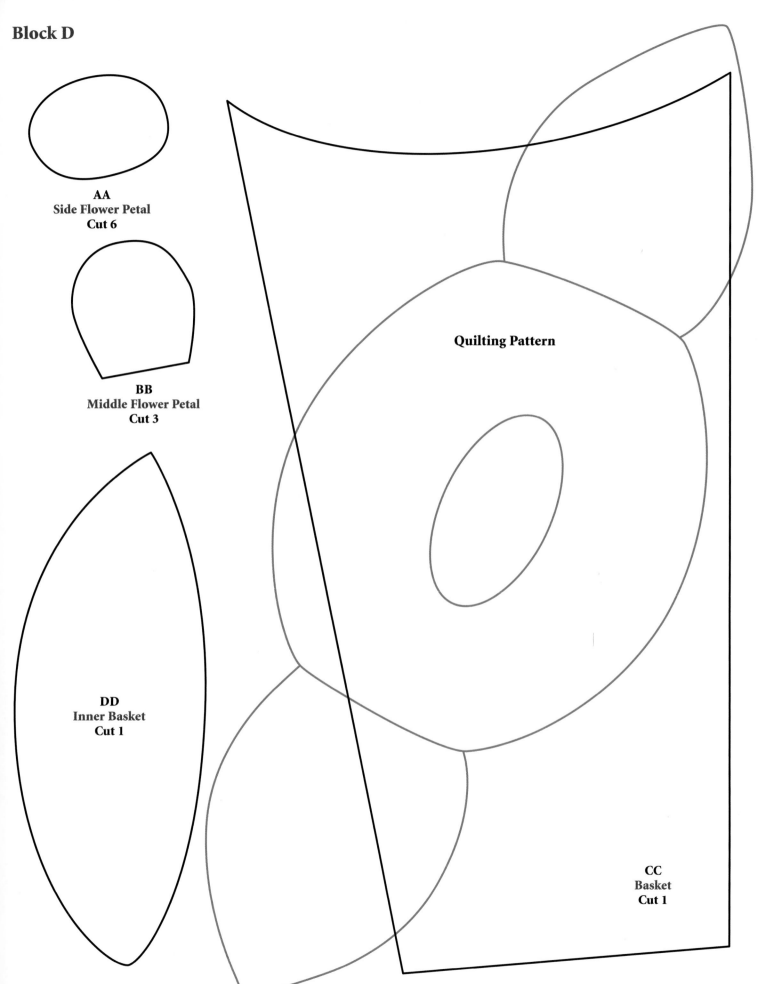

AA
Side Flower Petal
Cut 6

BB
Middle Flower Petal
Cut 3

DD
Inner Basket
Cut 1

Quilting Pattern

CC
Basket
Cut 1

31

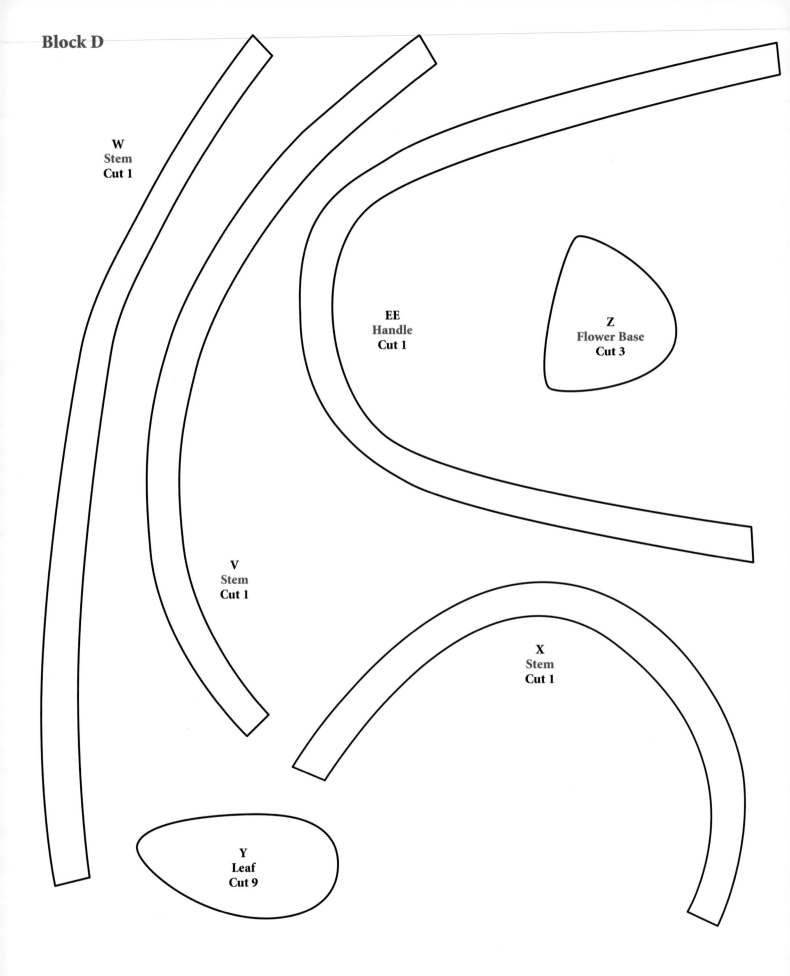

W
Stem
Cut 1

EE
Handle
Cut 1

Z
Flower Base
Cut 3

V
Stem
Cut 1

X
Stem
Cut 1

Y
Leaf
Cut 9

Block E

KK
Circle
Cut 9

FF
Leaf
Cut 2

OO
Flower Center
Cut 19

GG
Leaf
Cut 1

MM
Flower Center
Cut 7

LL
Flower
Cut 7

NN
Flower
Cut 19

HH
Leaf
Cut 2

II
Leaf
Cut 1

JJ
Leaf
Cut 2;
cut 1 in reverse.

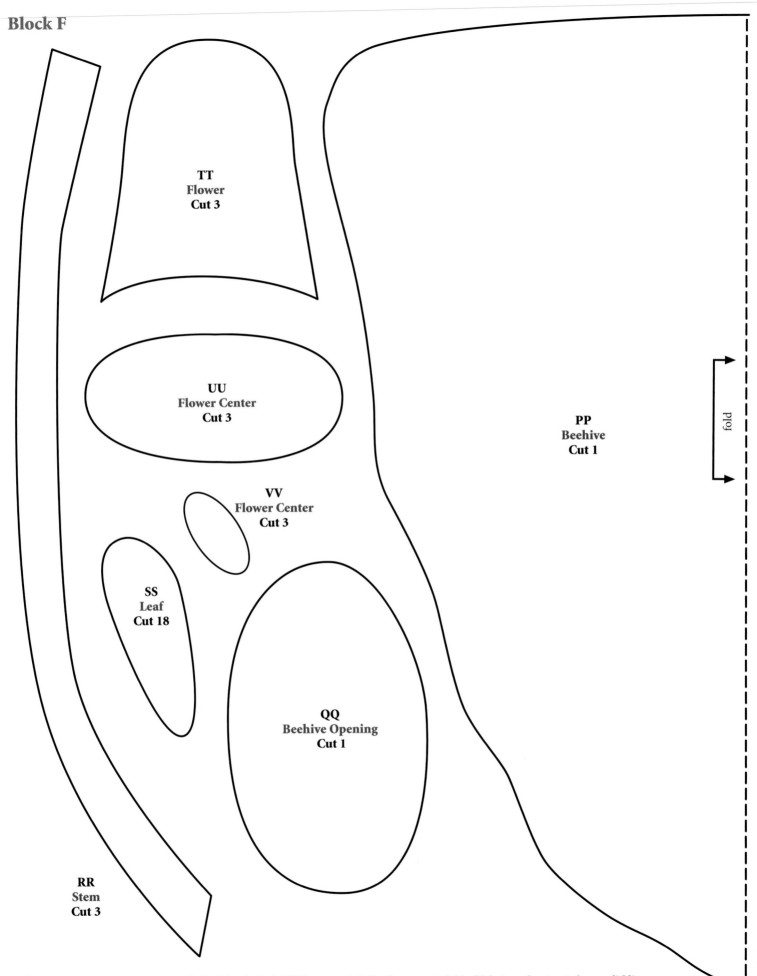

TT
Flower
Cut 3

UU
Flower Center
Cut 3

PP
Beehive
Cut 1

fold

VV
Flower Center
Cut 3

SS
Leaf
Cut 18

QQ
Beehive Opening
Cut 1

RR
Stem
Cut 3

NOTE: For patterns marked with a dashed fold line, match fold of pattern to fold of fabric and cut out along solid lines.

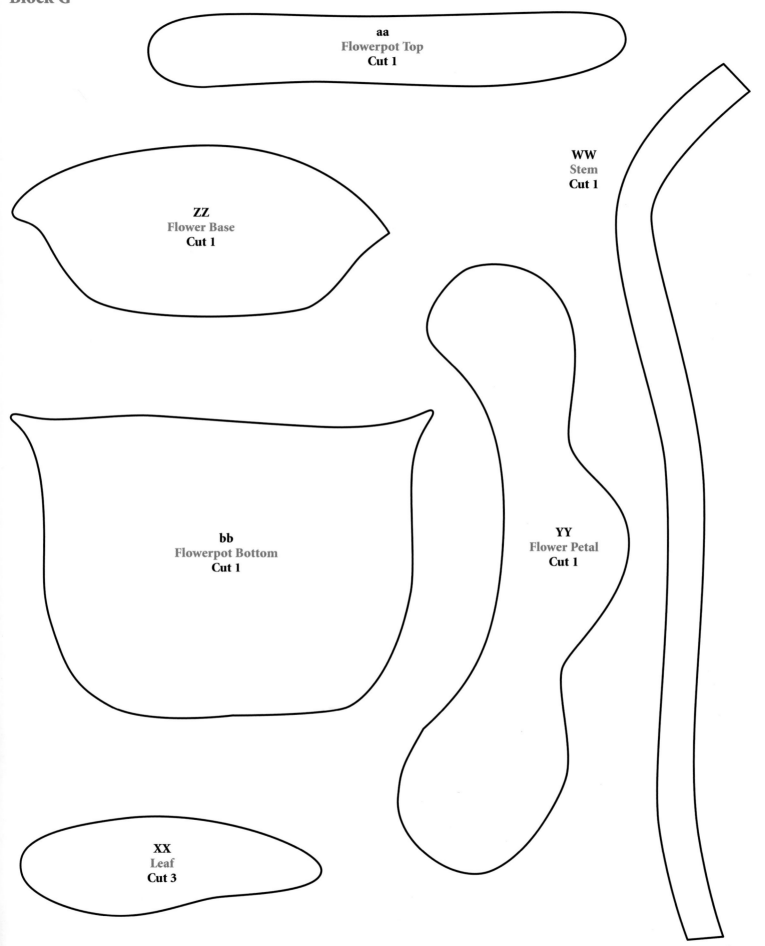

aa
Flowerpot Top
Cut 1

WW
Stem
Cut 1

ZZ
Flower Base
Cut 1

bb
Flowerpot Bottom
Cut 1

YY
Flower Petal
Cut 1

XX
Leaf
Cut 3

Grandma's
GARDEN

Both quilting and gardening require the artist to keep the best of the past — seeds or fabric scraps — and use them to create new works of beauty. The resulting flowerbed or quilt is the ultimate reward for a work of the heart. In this lovely composition, old and new fabrics are blended together to ensure that the sun will always shine on Grandma's Garden.

GRANDMA'S GARDEN
Finished Size: 60" x 67" (152 cm x 170 cm)

FABRIC REQUIREMENTS

$^5/_8$ yd (57 cm) **each** of 6 assorted prints for
   backgrounds
2 yds (1.8 m) of green print for inner borders
$^1/_4$ yd (23 cm) of blue print No. 1 for outer side
   border
$^1/_4$ yd (23 cm) of pink print No. 1 for outer side
border
2 yds (1.8 m) of white print No. 2 for top and
   bottom outer borders
$^1/_2$ yd (46 cm) **total** of assorted green prints
$^1/_4$ yd (23 cm) **total** of assorted yellow prints
$^1/_4$ yd (23 cm) **total** of assorted pink prints
$^1/_4$ yd (23 cm) **total** of assorted white prints
$^1/_8$ yd (11 cm) **total** of assorted purple prints
$^1/_8$ yd (11 cm) of blue print No. 2
$^1/_8$ yd (11 cm) **total** of assorted red prints
$^1/_2$ yd (46 cm) of binding fabric
$4^1/_4$ yds (3.9 m) of backing fabric
72" x 90" batting

CUTTING THE BACKGROUNDS AND BORDERS

*Yardage is based on 45"w fabric. Refer to **Rotary
Cutting**, page 101, before beginning project.*

From assorted prints:
  · Cut 6 background squares $17^1/_2$" x $17^1/_2$".

From green print:
  · Cut 2 lengthwise side inner borders $34^1/_2$" x 2".
  · Cut 2 lengthwise top and bottom inner borders
    $66^1/_2$" x 2".

From blue print No. 1:
  · Cut 1 lengthwise side outer border $34^1/_2$" x $6^1/_2$".

From pink print:
  · Cut 1 lengthwise side outer border $34^1/_2$" x $6^1/_2$".

From white print:
  · Cut 2 lengthwise top and bottom outer borders
    $66^1/_2$" x $11^1/_2$".

From binding fabric:
  · Cut 7 strips $2^1/_2$"w.

APPLIQUÉS

*Refer to **Making Templates**, page 104, to use patterns, pages 41-45, to make templates.* **Note:** *Appliqué patterns provided do not include seam allowances. Measurements given for bias strips include ¼" seam allowance.*

From assorted green prints:
- Cut 1 bias strip 1¼" x 12½" for stem (A).
- Cut 1 stem (B1, B2, and B3).
- Cut 2 small stems (C).
- Cut 1 bias strip 1¼" x 15½" for stem (D).
- Cut 1 bias strip 1¼" x 26" for stem (E).
- Cut 1 each of leaves (F, G, I, J, K, L, M, N, and O).
- Cut 2 leaves; cut 1 in reverse (H).
- Cut 3 buds (II).

From assorted white, pink, and purple prints:
- Cut 1 flower (P).
- Cut 3 flowers (R).
- Cut 3 flower parts (S).
- Cut 1 each of flowers (W, Y, and AA).
- Cut 2 each of flowers (CC, EE, and GG).
- Cut 1 each of flower centers (X, Z, and BB).
- Cut 2 each of flower centers (DD, FF, and HH).

From assorted red prints:
- Cut 1 flower center (Q).
- Cut 3 flower centers (T).

From blue print:
- Cut 1 flower (V).

From assorted yellow prints:
- Cut 1 sun (JJ) on fold.
- Cut 1 sunray (KK1 and KK2).
- Cut 1 flower center (U).

ASSEMBLING THE QUILT TOP

1. Refer to photo, page 38, and **Quilt Top Diagram**, page 40, for placement. Refer to **Piecing and Pressing**, page 103, to sew the 6 background squares together.
2. Refer to **Needle-Turn Appliqué**, page 104, for techniques. Working in alphabetical order, position pieces, then pin or baste in place and appliqué to make quilt top center.
3. Sew the side inner borders to the quilt top center, then add the side outer borders. Sew the top and bottom inner borders to the quilt top center, then the top and bottom outer borders.

FINISHING

1. Follow **Quilting**, page 106, to mark, layer, and quilt as desired. Our quilt was machine quilted.
2. Follow **Making Straight Grain Binding**, page 110, to make 7⅜ yds of 2½"w binding.
3. Refer to **Making a Hanging Sleeve**, page 111, to make and attach a hanging sleeve.
4. Follow **Attaching Binding with Mitered Corners**, page 110, to bind quilt.

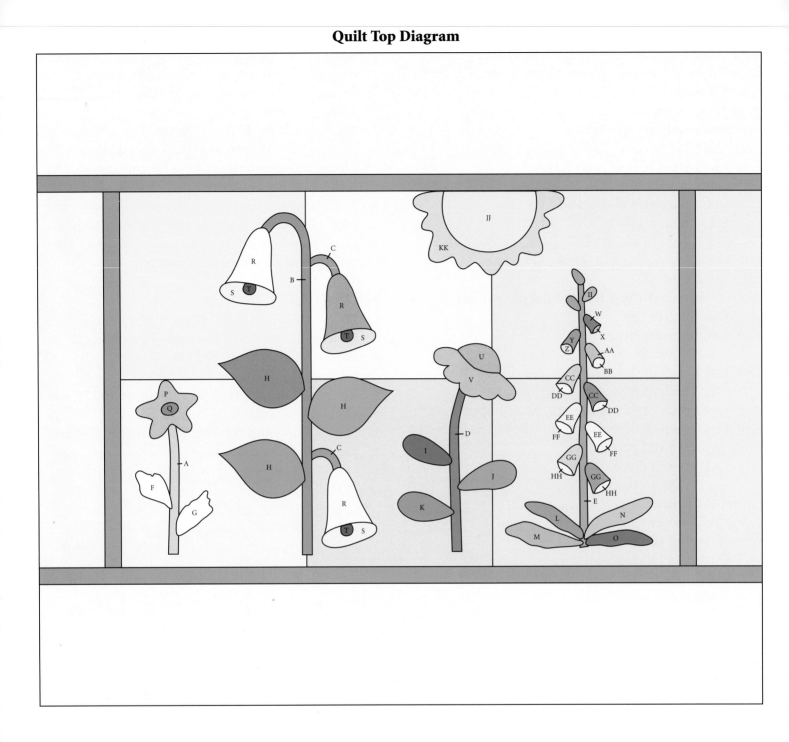

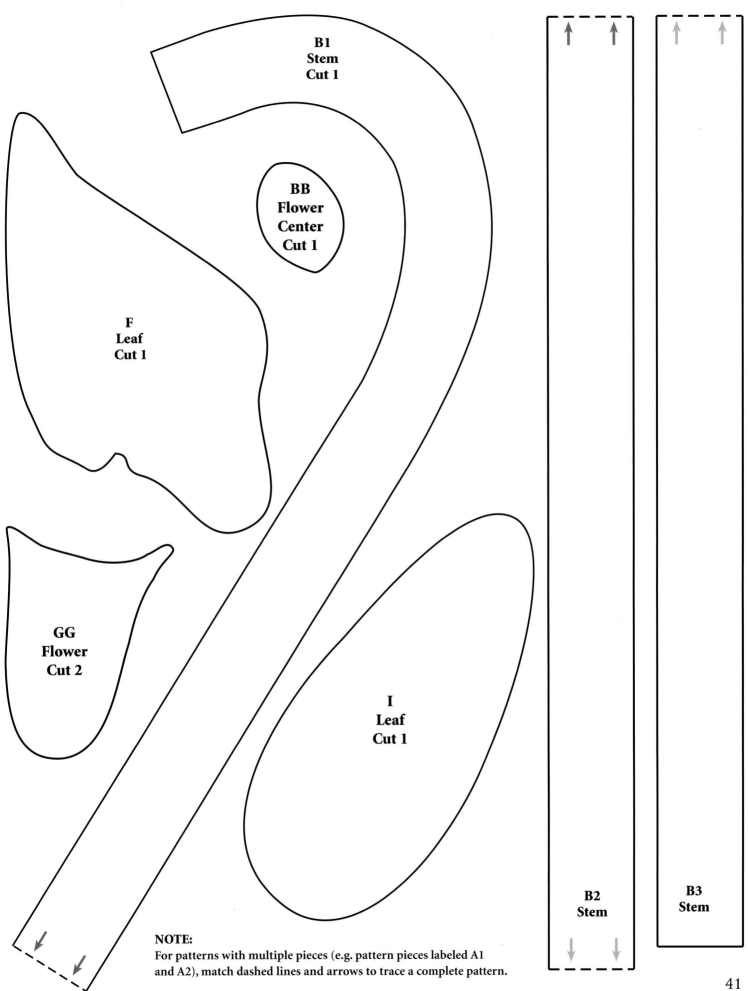

B1
Stem
Cut 1

BB
Flower
Center
Cut 1

F
Leaf
Cut 1

GG
Flower
Cut 2

I
Leaf
Cut 1

B2
Stem

B3
Stem

NOTE:
For patterns with multiple pieces (e.g. pattern pieces labeled A1
and A2), match dashed lines and arrows to trace a complete pattern.

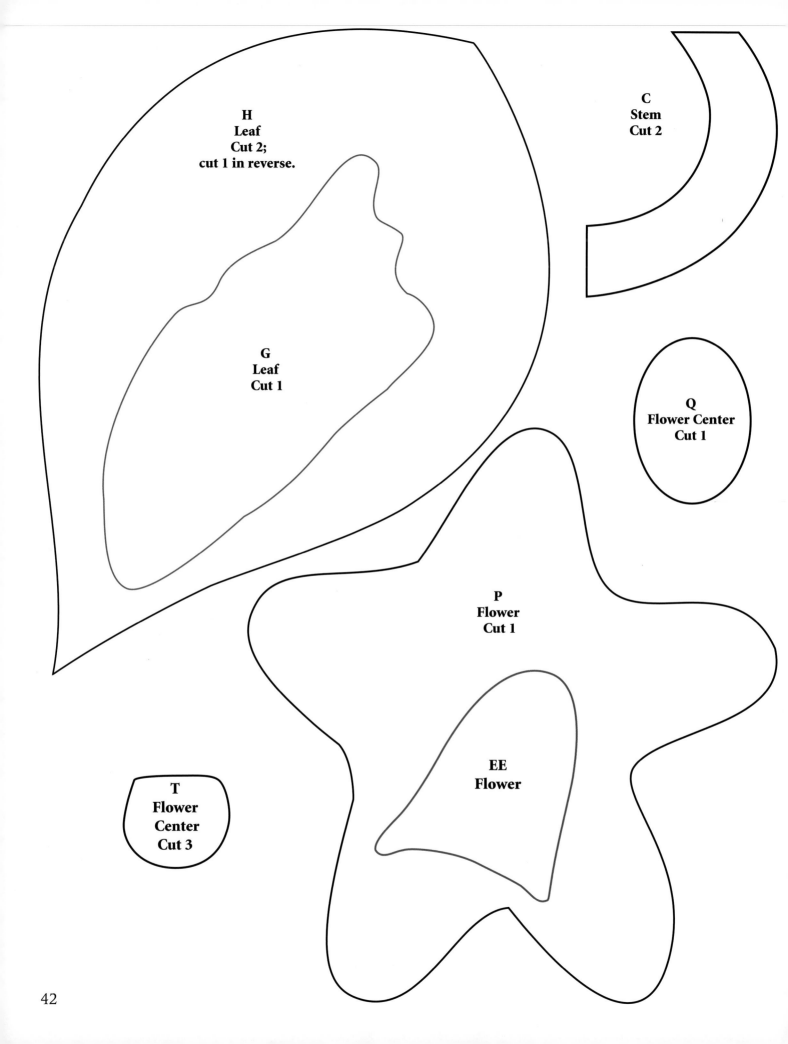

H
Leaf
Cut 2;
cut 1 in reverse.

C
Stem
Cut 2

G
Leaf
Cut 1

Q
Flower Center
Cut 1

P
Flower
Cut 1

T
Flower
Center
Cut 3

EE
Flower

42

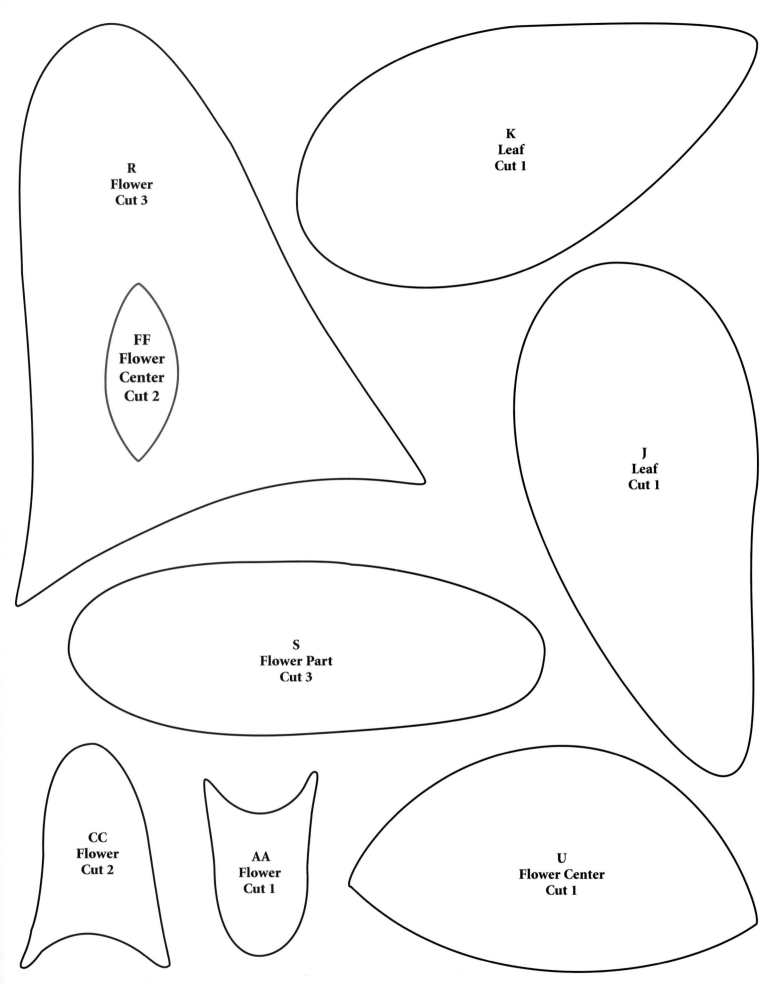

R
Flower
Cut 3

K
Leaf
Cut 1

FF
Flower
Center
Cut 2

J
Leaf
Cut 1

S
Flower Part
Cut 3

CC
Flower
Cut 2

AA
Flower
Cut 1

U
Flower Center
Cut 1

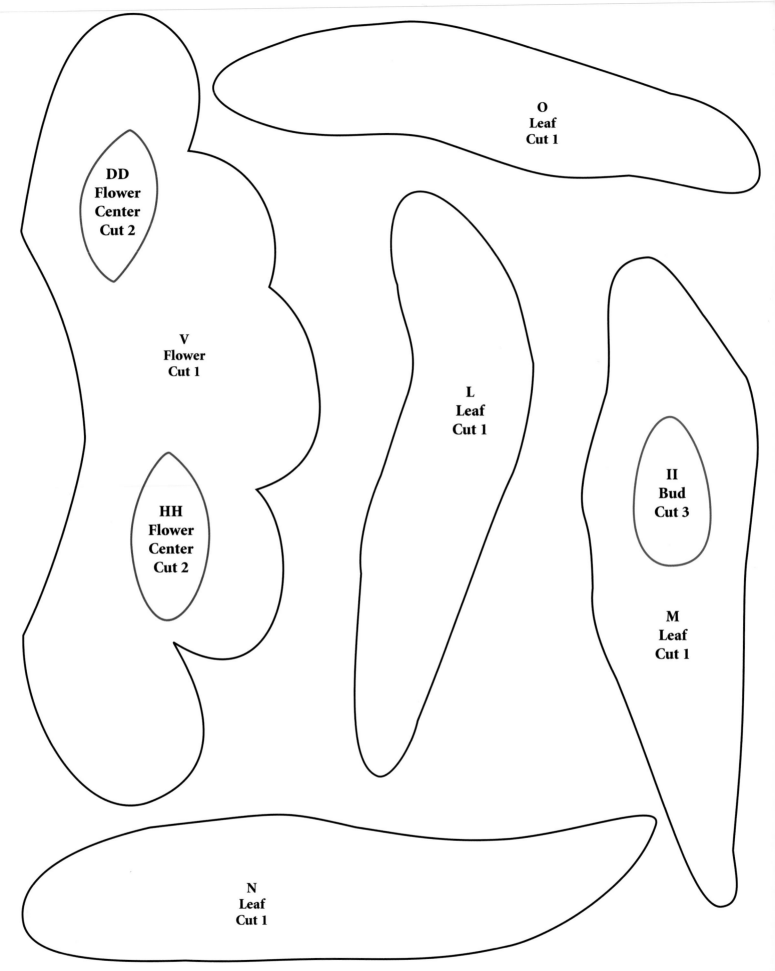

O
Leaf
Cut 1

DD
Flower
Center
Cut 2

V
Flower
Cut 1

L
Leaf
Cut 1

II
Bud
Cut 3

M
Leaf
Cut 1

HH
Flower
Center
Cut 2

N
Leaf
Cut 1

44

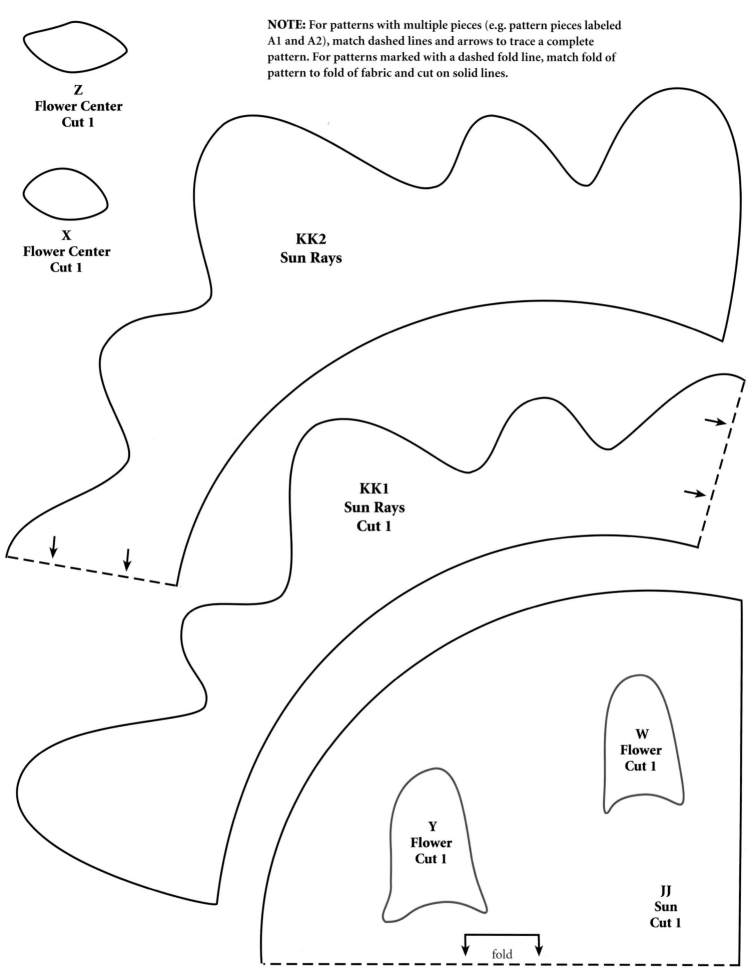

NOTE: For patterns with multiple pieces (e.g. pattern pieces labeled A1 and A2), match dashed lines and arrows to trace a complete pattern. For patterns marked with a dashed fold line, match fold of pattern to fold of fabric and cut on solid lines.

Z
Flower Center
Cut 1

X
Flower Center
Cut 1

KK2
Sun Rays

KK1
Sun Rays
Cut 1

W
Flower
Cut 1

Y
Flower
Cut 1

JJ
Sun
Cut 1

fold

Rainbow SHERBET

Which is more refreshing: the name of this quilt, or the three-dimensional quality of its fabulous blooms? Feedsack scraps and reproduction fabric melt together to create a delicious summertime confection. Indulge!

RAINBOW SHERBET

Finished Size: 49" x 60" (124 cm x 152 cm)

FABRIC REQUIREMENTS

$1^5/8$ yds (1.5 m) of yellow fabric

$5/8$ yd (57 cm) of pink fabric

$1/2$ yd (46 cm) **total** of assorted green prints

$1^1/2$ yds (1.4 m) **total** of assorted pink, blue, purple, yellow, and red prints

$1/2$ yd (46 cm) of binding fabric

3 yds (2.7 m) of backing fabric

72" x 90" batting

Twenty-one $3/4$" diameter buttons of assorted colors

CUTTING THE BACKGROUNDS AND BLOCKS

Yardage is based on 45"w fabric. Refer to **Rotary Cutting**, *page 101, before beginning project.*

From yellow fabric:

· Cut 3 background rectangles (No. 1) $12^1/2$" x $42^1/2$".

· Cut 4 background rectangles (No. 2) $11^3/4$" x 9".

From pink fabric:

· Cut 6 squares (No. 3) $6^1/2$" x $6^1/2$".

· Cut 12 squares $5^1/8$" x $5^1/8$". Cut squares in half diagonally to make 24 triangles (No. 4).

From light-colored print:

· Cut 14 squares (No. 5) $2^1/2$" x $2^1/2$".

From assorted pink, red, blue, green, yellow, and purple prints:

· Cut 56 rectangles (No. 6) $2^1/2$" x $4^1/2$".

From binding fabric:

· Cut 6 strips $2^1/2$"w.

CUTTING THE APPLIQUÉS

*Refer to **Making Templates**, page 104, to use patterns, pages 52-53, to make templates. **Note:** Appliqué patterns provided do not include seam allowances. Measurements given for dimensional flowers and bias strips include ¹/₄" seam allowance. To help keep blocks organized, lay out all appliqué pieces with corresponding backgrounds as you cut.*

Block A

From assorted green prints:
- Cut 1 bias strip 1¹/₄" x 37" for vine (A).
- Cut 1 small leaf (B).
- Cut 2 large leaves (C).

From assorted prints:
- Cut 4 large flowers (D).
- Cut 5 small flowers (E).

Block B

From assorted green prints:
- Cut 1 bias strip 1¹/₄" x 37" for vine (F).
- Cut 3 leaves on fold (G).

From assorted pink, blue, purple, and red prints:
- Cut 16 flowers (2 each of 8 prints) on fold (H).

Block C

From assorted green prints:
- Cut 1 bias strip 1¹/₄" x 37" for vine (I).
- Cut 2 leaves (C).

From assorted prints:
- Cut 4 flowers (D).
- Cut 4 squares 2¹/₂" x 2¹/₂" for flower centers (J).

Block D

From assorted green prints:
- Cut 8 leaves on fold (K).

From assorted blue, pink, and yellow prints:
- Cut 8 flowers (2 each of 4 prints) on fold (L).

MAKING THE BLOCKS

*Refer to **Piecing and Pressing**, page 103, and **Needle-Turn Appliqué**, page 104, to assemble the blocks. Refer to **Quilt Top Diagram**, page 51, and **Block Diagrams** for placement. Working in alphabetical order, position pieces, then pin or baste in place on background rectangle before appliquéing.*

Blocks A and C

1. Appliqué stem, leaves, and flowers on a No. 1 background rectangle as shown.
2. Sew a button in the center of each appliquéd flower.

Block A Diagram   **Block C Diagram**

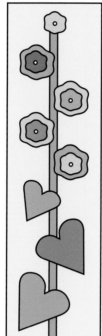 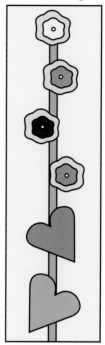

Block B

1. Appliqué stem and leaves on a No. 1 background rectangle.
2. Matching right sides and raw edges and leaving an opening for turning, sew flower pieces (H) together. Turn flower right side out and blind stitch opening closed. Fold flower in half and sew a small pleat on back approximately ¹/₂" from center fold (**Fig. 1**). Make 8 flowers.

Fig. 1

3. Position flowers on stem and sew in place with a button.

Block B Diagram

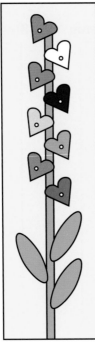

Block D

1. Matching right sides and raw edges and leaving an opening for turning, sew flower pieces (L) together. Turn flower right side out and blind stitch opening closed. Fold flower in half and sew a small pleat on back approximately $1/2$" from center fold (**Fig. 2**). Make 4 flowers.

Fig. 2

2. Position flower at the center of a No. 2 background rectangle and sew in place with a button.

3. Refer to photo to position leaves, then pin or baste in place and appliqué.

Block D Diagram

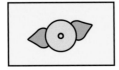

Block E

1. Refer to **Block E Diagram** to piece the No. 5 square and the No. 6 strips together in the order shown.

2. To sew strip b to square, mark a dot $1/4$" in from one corner of the square. With right sides together and matching raw edges, stitch the seam from the outer edge to the dot, backstitching at dot (**Fig. 3**). Press seam.

Fig. 3

3. Sew strips c and d to square as shown.

4. To sew strip e to square and strip d, mark a dot $1/4$" in from one corner of strip e. With right sides together, match dot on strip to dot on square. Sew strip from outer edge to dot, backstitching at dot (**Fig. 4**). Press seam.

Fig. 4

5. Fold strip b back over square and strip e. Matching raw edges, complete the first seam to make **Block E**. Make 14 **Block E's** (6 blocks will be used for **Block F**).

Block E Diagram

Block F

Referring to **Block Diagram** for placement, sew 4 No. 4 pink triangles to **Block E** as shown to make **Block F**. Trim finished block to measure $8^1/2$" x $8^1/2$". Make 6 **Block F's**.

Block F Diagram

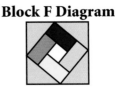

ASSEMBLING THE QUILT TOP

Referring to photo, page 48, and **Quilt Top Diagram** for placement, sew the blocks together in the order listed below.

1. Sew 4 **Block E's** and 3 No. 3 squares together to make **Unit 1**. Make 2 **Unit 1's**.
2. Sew 2 **Unit 1's** and **Block A**, **Block B**, and **Block C** together to make **Unit 2**.
3. Sew 3 **Block F's** and 2 **Block D's** together to make **Unit 3**. Make 2 **Unit 3's**.

4. Sew a **Unit 3** to the top and bottom of **Unit 2** to make quilt top.

FINISHING

1. Follow **Quilting**, page 106, to mark, layer, and quilt as desired. Our quilt was machine quilted.
2. Follow **Making Straight Grain Binding**, page 110, to make 6³/₈ yds of 2¹/₂"w binding.
3. Follow **Attaching Binding with Mitered Corners**, page 110, to bind quilt.

Quilt Top Diagram

51

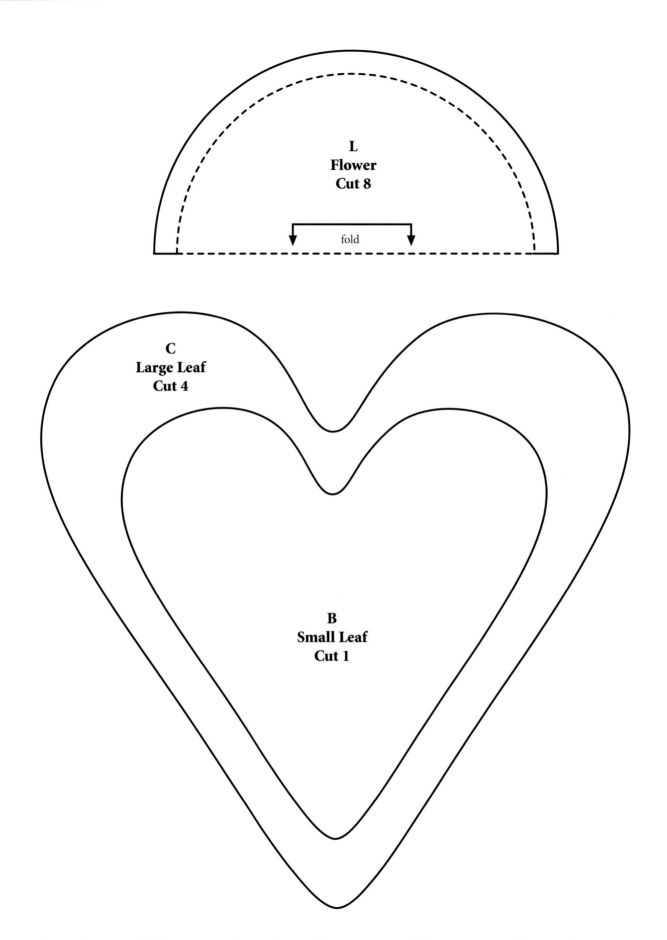

L
Flower
Cut 8

fold

C
Large Leaf
Cut 4

B
Small Leaf
Cut 1

NOTE: For patterns marked with a dashed fold line, match fold of pattern to fold of fabric and cut on solid lines.

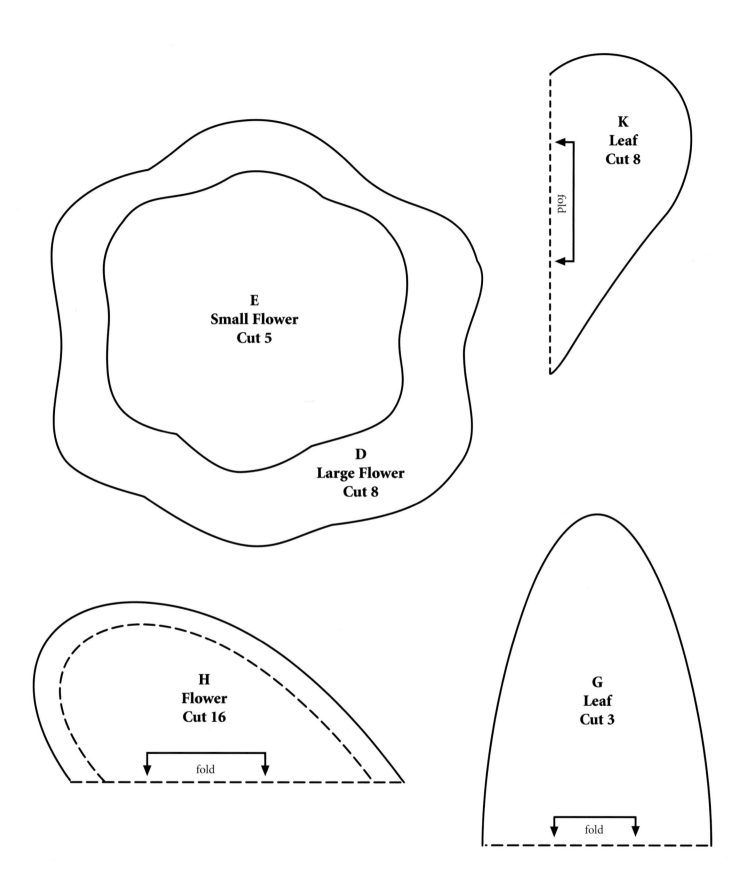

K
Leaf
Cut 8

fold

E
Small Flower
Cut 5

D
Large Flower
Cut 8

H
Flower
Cut 16

fold

G
Leaf
Cut 3

fold

Spring BASKETS

While dew still sparkles on your garden, gather flowers by the basketful... six baskets full, to be precise. Appliquéd to blocks that are framed with colorful fabric strips, these fresh cuttings will brighten your home for many years to come. And the vining blossoms on the border? Needle-turn appliqué makes them just "glory-ous."

SPRING BASKETS
Finished Size: 55" x 73" (140 cm x 185 cm)

FABRIC REQUIREMENTS

$^1/_2$ yd (46 cm) of beige print No. 1
$^1/_2$ yd (46 cm) of beige print No. 2
$^1/_2$ yd (46 cm) of pink print No. 1
$^3/_8$ yd (34 cm) of pink print No. 2
$^7/_8$ yd (80 cm) of yellow print No. 1
$^7/_8$ yd (80 cm) of yellow print No. 2
$^3/_8$ yd (34 cm) of green print for border blocks
1 yd (91 cm) **total** of assorted pink, yellow, and green prints for sashings
$1^1/_2$ yds (1.4 m) **total** of assorted green prints for vines, stems, and leaves
$^1/_4$ yd (23 cm) **total** of assorted yellow prints
$^1/_4$ yd (23 cm) of tan print
$^3/_4$ yd (69 cm) **total** of assorted pink prints
Scraps of assorted purple and blue prints
$^1/_2$ yd (46 cm) of binding fabric
$3^1/_2$ yds (3.0 m) of backing fabric
72" x 90" batting

CUTTING THE BACKGROUNDS AND BORDERS

Yardage is based on 45"w fabric. Refer to **Rotary Cutting***, page 101, before beginning project. To help keep pieces organized, refer to photo and* **Unit Diagrams** *to lay out the pieces as you cut.*

From beige print No. 1:
  · Cut 1 background square (No. 1) $14^1/_2$" x $14^1/_2$".
  · Cut 1 background square (No. 2) $15^1/_2$" x $15^1/_2$".
From beige print No. 2:
  · Cut 1 background rectangle (No. 3) $18^1/_2$" x $10^1/_2$".
  · Cut 1 background square (No. 4) $15^1/_2$" x $15^1/_2$".
From pink print No. 1:
  · Cut 1 background square (No. 5) $14^1/_2$" x $14^1/_2$".
  · Cut 1 background rectangle (No. 6) $18^1/_2$" x $13^1/_2$".
From pink print No. 2:
  · Cut 2 border rectangles (Nos. 7 and 8) $9^1/_2$" x $18^1/_2$".
From yellow print No. 1:
  · Cut 2 border rectangles (Nos. 9 and 10) $27^1/_2$" x $9^1/_2$".
From yellow print No. 2:
  · Cut 2 border rectangles (Nos. 11 and 12) $27^1/_2$" x $9^1/_2$".
  · Cut 2 border rectangles (Nos. 13 and 14) $9^1/_2$" x $18^1/_2$".

From green print:
- Cut 2 border rectangles (Nos. 15 and 16) $9^1/2$" x $18^1/2$".

From assorted pink, yellow, and green prints:
- Cut 1 sashing strip (No. 17) $18^1/2$" x $1^1/2$".
- Cut 8 sashing strips (Nos. 18-25) 2" x 17".
- Cut 2 sashing strips (Nos. 26 and 27) $18^1/2$" x 2".
- Cut 1 sashing strip (No. 28) $4^1/2$" x $2^1/2$".
- Cut 1 sashing strip (No. 29) $8^1/2$" x $2^1/2$".
- Cut 1 sashing strip (No. 30) $6^1/2$" x $2^1/2$".
- Cut 8 sashing strips (Nos. 31-38) $2^1/2$" x $16^1/2$".
- Cut 1 sashing strip (No. 39) $18^1/2$" x $2^1/2$".
- Cut 2 sashing strips (Nos. 40 and 41) $18^1/2$" x 3".

From binding fabric:
- Cut 7 strips $2^1/2$"w.

CUTTING THE APPLIQUÉS

*Refer to **Making Templates**, page 104, to use patterns, pages 61-69, to make templates. **Note:** Appliqué patterns provided do not include seam allowances. Measurements given for rectangles and bias strips include a $1/4$" seam allowance. To help keep blocks organized, lay out all appliqué pieces with corresponding backgrounds as you cut.*

Block A

From assorted pink prints:
- Cut 1 inside basket piece (A).
- Cut 1 handle (B).
- Cut 3 flowers (J).
- Cut 1 left basket (K).
- Cut 1 right basket (L).

From 1 green print:
- Cut 1 each of stems (C, D, and E).
- Cut 1 each of leaves (F, G, H, and I).

Block B

From assorted pink prints:
- Cut 1 inside basket (M).
- Cut 1 handle on fold (N).
- Cut 1 basket on fold (O).
- Cut 2 flowers (P).

From tan print:
- Cut 1 flower center (Q).

From purple print:
- Cut 1 flower (P).

From assorted green prints:
- Cut 1 flower center (Q).
- Cut 6 leaves (R).

From yellow print:
- Cut 1 flower center (Q).

Block C

From assorted green prints:
- Cut 1 each of stems (X, Y, Z, and AA).
- Cut 8 leaves (CC).

From blue prints:
- Cut 2 flowers (BB).

From assorted pink prints:
- Cut 1 plate (S).
- Cut 1 plate rim (T1 and T2).
- Cut 1 bowl (U).
- Cut 1 inside bowl (V).
- Cut 1 bowl rim on fold (W).
- Cut 2 flowers (BB).

Block D

From tan print:
- Cut 1 basket (DD).
- Cut 1 right handle (FF).
- Cut 1 basket top (GG).
- Cut 1 basket bottom (HH).

From assorted pink prints:
- Cut 1 left handle (EE).
- Cut 1 each of flowers (KK and MM).

From assorted green prints:
- Cut 3 large leaves (II).
- Cut 2 small leaves (JJ).

From yellow print:
- Cut 1 each of flower centers (LL and NN).

Block E

From assorted pink prints:
- Cut 1 rectangle 12" x $4^1/4$" for basket (OO).
- Cut 1 rectangle $13^1/2$" x $1^1/4$" for basket top (WW).
- Cut 1 each of flowers (g, h, j, k, and n).
- Cut 1 each of flower centers (o and q).

From assorted purple prints:
- Cut 1 each of flowers (m and p).
- Cut 1 each of flower centers (i and l).

From assorted green prints:
- Cut 1 each of stems (PP, QQ, RR, SS, TT, UU, and VV).
- Cut 1 each of leaves (XX, YY, ZZ, a, b, c, d, e, and f).

Block F

From assorted pink prints:
- Cut 1 inside pitcher (r).
- Cut 1 handle (t).
- Cut 6 flowers (z).
- Cut 6 flower centers (aa).

From yellow print:
- Cut 1 pitcher (s).

From 1 green print:
- Cut 1 stem (u).
- Cut 1 each of leaves (v, w, x, and y).

Border Vines

From assorted pink, purple, and yellow prints:
- Cut 16 flowers (bb).
- Cut 16 flower centers (cc).

From assorted green prints:
- Cut 4 bias strips 1" x 62" (dd) for vines.
- Cut 32 leaves (ee).

MAKING THE UNITS

*Refer to **Piecing and Pressing**, page 103, and **Needle-Turn Appliqué**, page 104, to assemble the blocks. Refer to **Unit Diagram** and photo, page 56, for placement. Working in alphabetical order, position pieces, then pin or baste in place on background rectangle or square before appliquéing.*

Unit 1

1. Appliqué pieces on No. 1 background square to make **Block A**.
2. To sew sashing strips (Nos. 31, 32, 33, and 34) to **Block A**, mark a dot on the wrong side of block $1/4$" in from each corner and at one corner of each sashing strip (**Fig. 1**).

Fig. 1

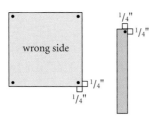

3. Matching right sides, pin the first strip to the block as shown. Stitch seam from outer edge to dot, backstitching at dot (**Fig. 2**). Press seam open.

Fig. 2

4. For next strip, match right sides and dots; pin in place. Stitch seam from dot to dot (**Fig. 3**). Press seam open.

Fig. 3

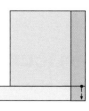

5. Fold first strip back over block and second strip. Matching raw edges of strips, complete the first seam (**Fig. 4**).

Fig. 4

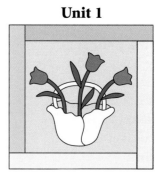

6. Repeat **Steps 4** and **5** for remaining 2 sashing strips to complete **Unit 1**.

Unit 1

Unit 2

1. Appliqué pieces on No. 3 background rectangle to make **Block B**.
2. Sew sashing strips (Nos. 17, 26, and 27) to the top of the block.
3. Sew sashing strips (Nos. 28, 29, and 30) together to make an $18^{1}/_{2}$" x $2^{1}/_{2}$" strip.
4. Sew pieced sashing strip and sashing strip (No. 39) to the bottom of the block to make **Unit 2**.

Unit 2

Unit 3

1. Appliqué pieces on No. 4 background square to make **Block C**.
2. Refer to **Block A, Steps 2-6,** to sew sashing strips (Nos. 18, 19, 20, and 21) to **Block C** to make **Unit 3**.

Unit 3

Unit 4

1. Appliqué pieces on No. 5 background square to make **Block D**.
2. Refer to **Block A, Steps 2-6,** to sew sashing strips (Nos. 35, 36, 37, and 38) to **Block D** to make **Unit 4**.

Unit 4

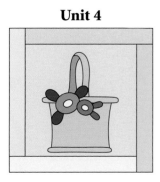

Unit 5

1. Appliqué pieces on No. 6 background rectangle to make **Block E**.
2. Sew No. 40 sashing strip to the top and No. 41 sashing strip to the bottom of **Block E** to make **Unit 5**.

Unit 5

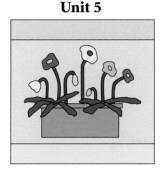

Unit 6

1. Appliqué pieces on No. 2 background square to make **Block F**.
2. Refer to **Block A, Steps 2-6,** to sew sashing strips (Nos. 22, 23, 24, and 25) to **Block F** to make **Unit 6**.

Unit 6

Assembling the Quilt Top

Referring to the **Quilt Top Diagram**, page 60, and photo, page 56, for placement, sew **Units 1 - 6** together to make quilt top center.

Adding the Borders

*Referring to **Quilt Top Diagram**, page 60, and photo, page 56, for placement, sew the border rectangles together in the order listed below.*

1. Sew border rectangles No. 13, No. 7, and No. 16 together to make left side border.
2. Sew border rectangles No. 15, No. 14, and No. 8 together to make right side border.
3. Sew border rectangle No. 9 to No. 11 to make top border.
4. Sew border rectangle No. 12 to No. 10 to make bottom border.
5. Sew side borders, then top and bottom borders to quilt top center.
6. Appliqué 1 vine (dd), 4 flowers (bb), 4 flower centers (cc), and 8 leaves (hh) to each border to make quilt top.

FINISHING

1. Follow **Quilting**, page 106, to mark, layer, and quilt, as desired. Our quilt was hand quilted.
2. Follow **Making Straight Grain Binding**, page 110, to make $7^{1}/_{2}$ yds of $2^{1}/_{2}$"w binding.
3. Follow **Attaching Binding with Mitered Corners**, page 110, to bind quilt.

Block A

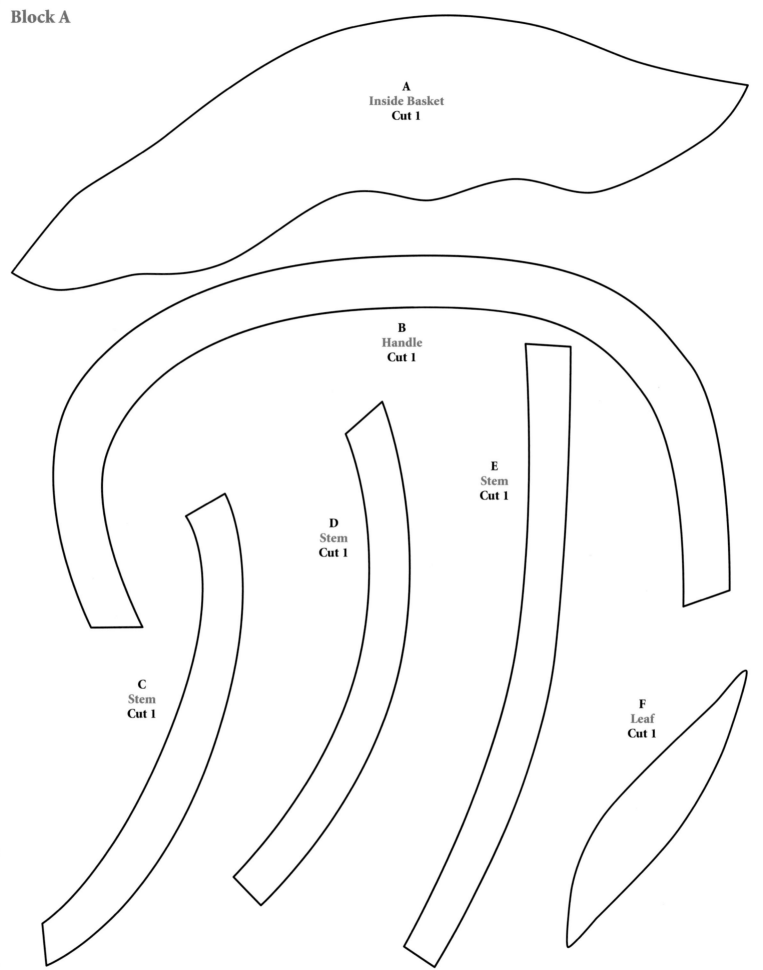

A
Inside Basket
Cut 1

B
Handle
Cut 1

E
Stem
Cut 1

D
Stem
Cut 1

C
Stem
Cut 1

F
Leaf
Cut 1

61

Block A

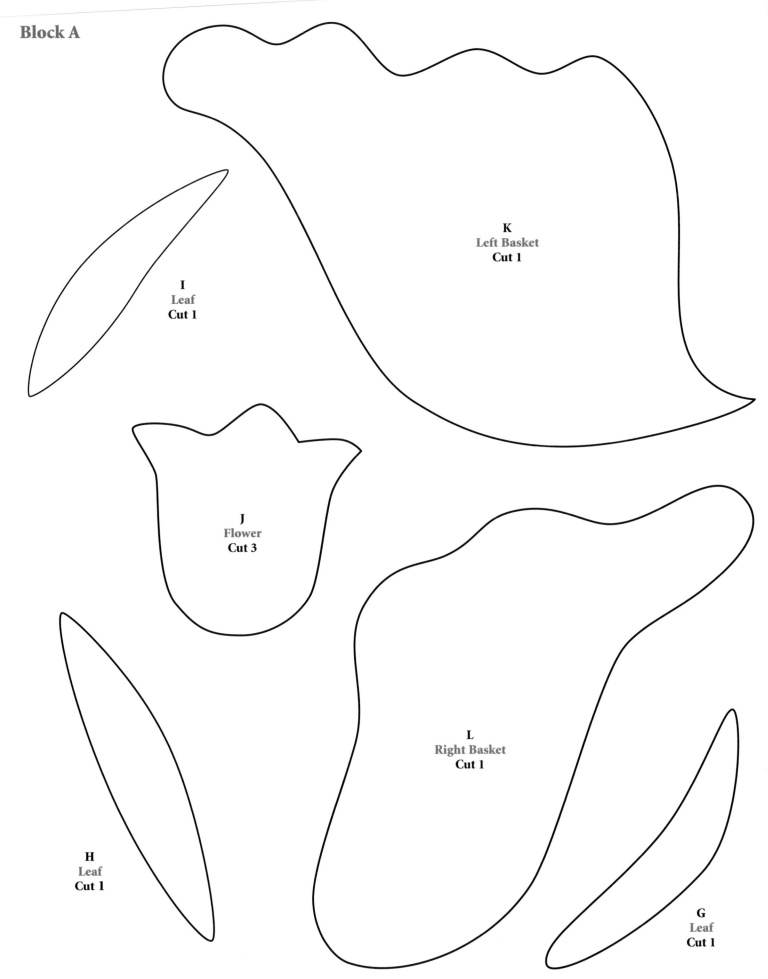

K
Left Basket
Cut 1

I
Leaf
Cut 1

J
Flower
Cut 3

L
Right Basket
Cut 1

H
Leaf
Cut 1

G
Leaf
Cut 1

Block B
NOTE: For patterns marked wih a dashed fold line, match fold of pattern to fold of fabric and cut out along solid lines.

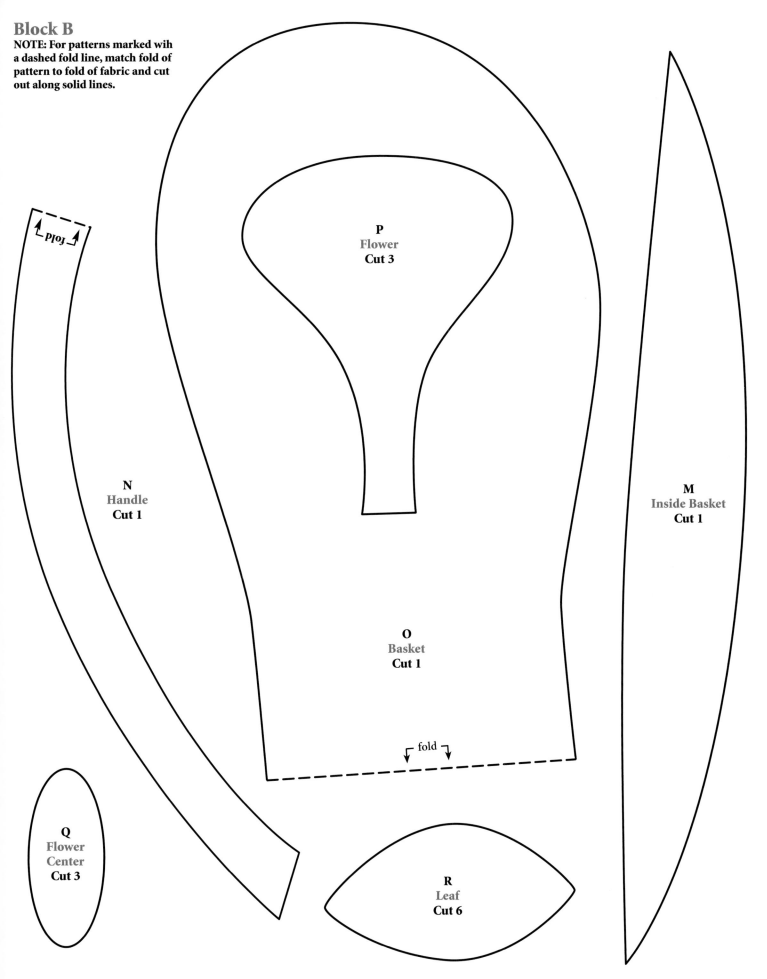

fold

N
Handle
Cut 1

P
Flower
Cut 3

M
Inside Basket
Cut 1

O
Basket
Cut 1

fold

Q
Flower
Center
Cut 3

R
Leaf
Cut 6

Block C

NOTE: For patterns with multiple pieces (e/g: pattern pieces labeled A1 and A2), match dashed lines and arrows to trace a complete pattern. For patterns marked wih a dashed fold line, match fold of pattern to fold of fabric and cut out along solid lines.

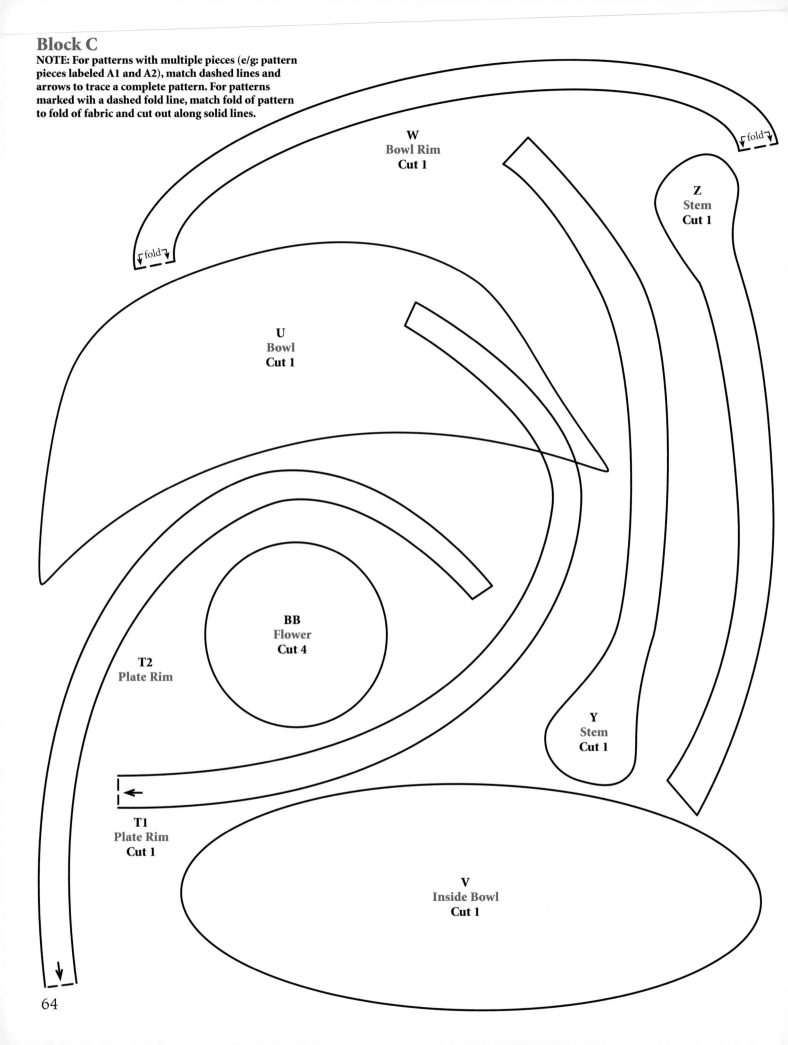

W
Bowl Rim
Cut 1

fold

Z
Stem
Cut 1

fold

U
Bowl
Cut 1

BB
Flower
Cut 4

T2
Plate Rim

Y
Stem
Cut 1

T1
Plate Rim
Cut 1

V
Inside Bowl
Cut 1

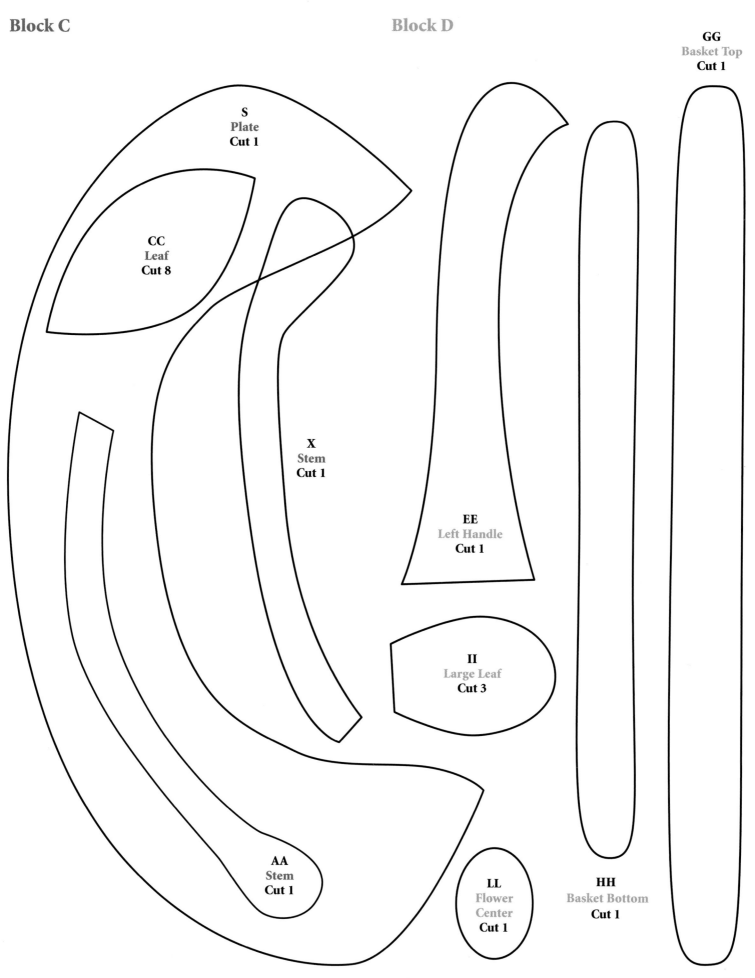

Block C

Block D

GG
Basket Top
Cut 1

S
Plate
Cut 1

CC
Leaf
Cut 8

X
Stem
Cut 1

EE
Left Handle
Cut 1

II
Large Leaf
Cut 3

AA
Stem
Cut 1

LL
Flower
Center
Cut 1

HH
Basket Bottom
Cut 1

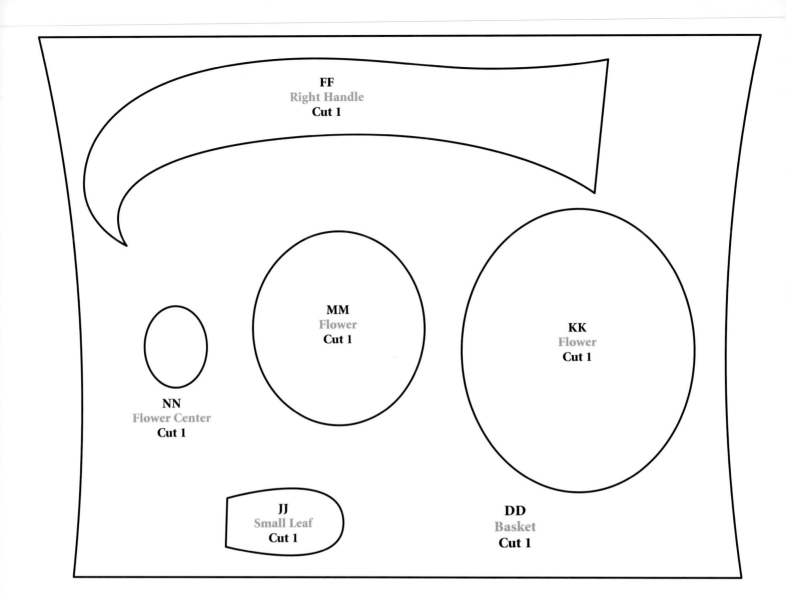

FF
Right Handle
Cut 1

MM
Flower
Cut 1

KK
Flower
Cut 1

NN
Flower Center
Cut 1

JJ
Small Leaf
Cut 1

DD
Basket
Cut 1

Border Vines

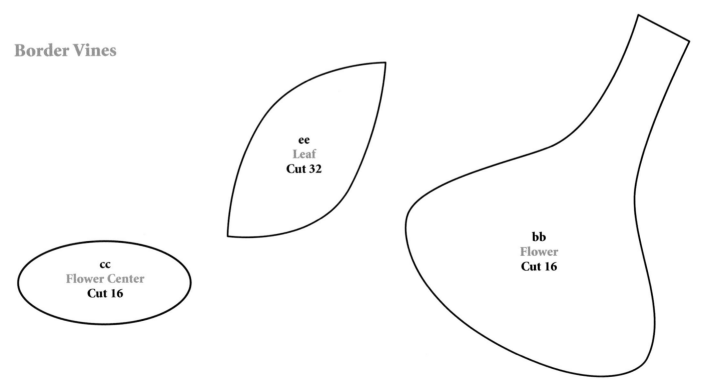

ee
Leaf
Cut 32

bb
Flower
Cut 16

cc
Flower Center
Cut 16

Block E

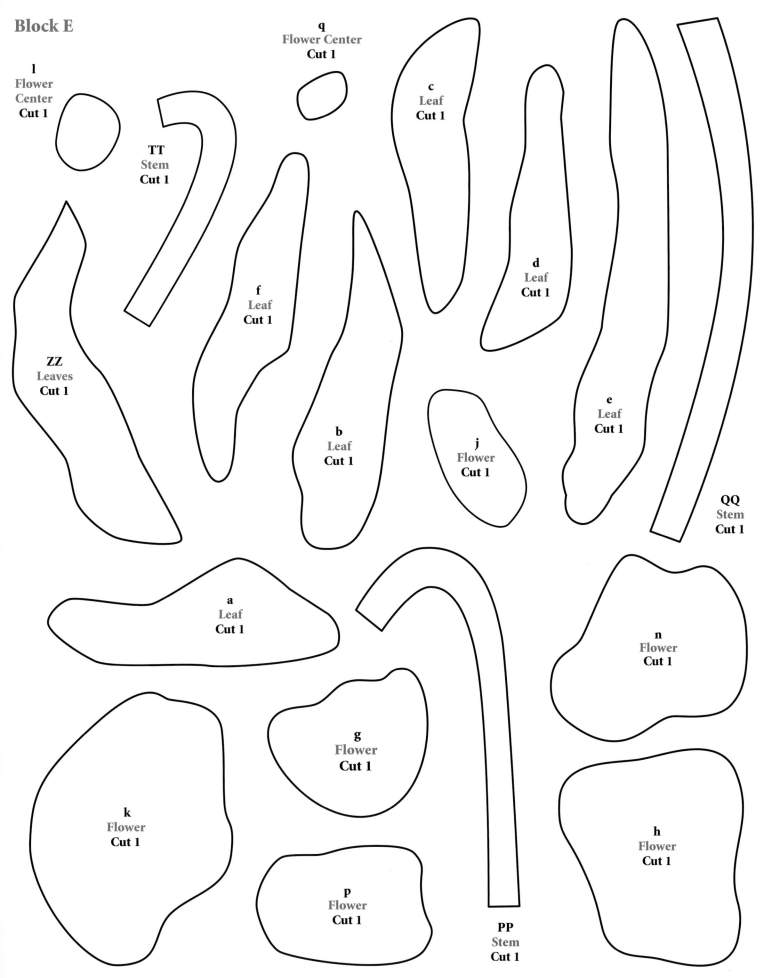

l
Flower
Center
Cut 1

q
Flower Center
Cut 1

c
Leaf
Cut 1

TT
Stem
Cut 1

ZZ
Leaves
Cut 1

f
Leaf
Cut 1

d
Leaf
Cut 1

b
Leaf
Cut 1

j
Flower
Cut 1

e
Leaf
Cut 1

QQ
Stem
Cut 1

a
Leaf
Cut 1

n
Flower
Cut 1

k
Flower
Cut 1

g
Flower
Cut 1

p
Flower
Cut 1

PP
Stem
Cut 1

h
Flower
Cut 1

67

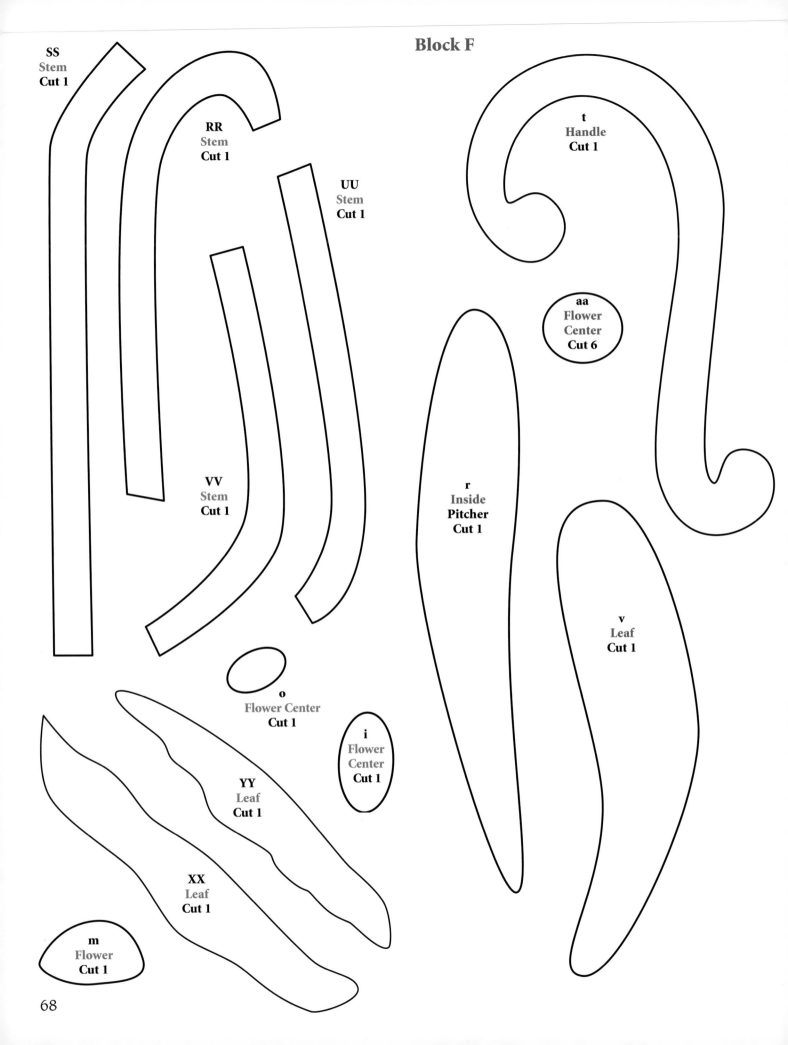

Block F

SS
Stem
Cut 1

RR
Stem
Cut 1

UU
Stem
Cut 1

t
Handle
Cut 1

aa
Flower
Center
Cut 6

VV
Stem
Cut 1

r
Inside
Pitcher
Cut 1

v
Leaf
Cut 1

o
Flower Center
Cut 1

i
Flower
Center
Cut 1

YY
Leaf
Cut 1

XX
Leaf
Cut 1

m
Flower
Cut 1

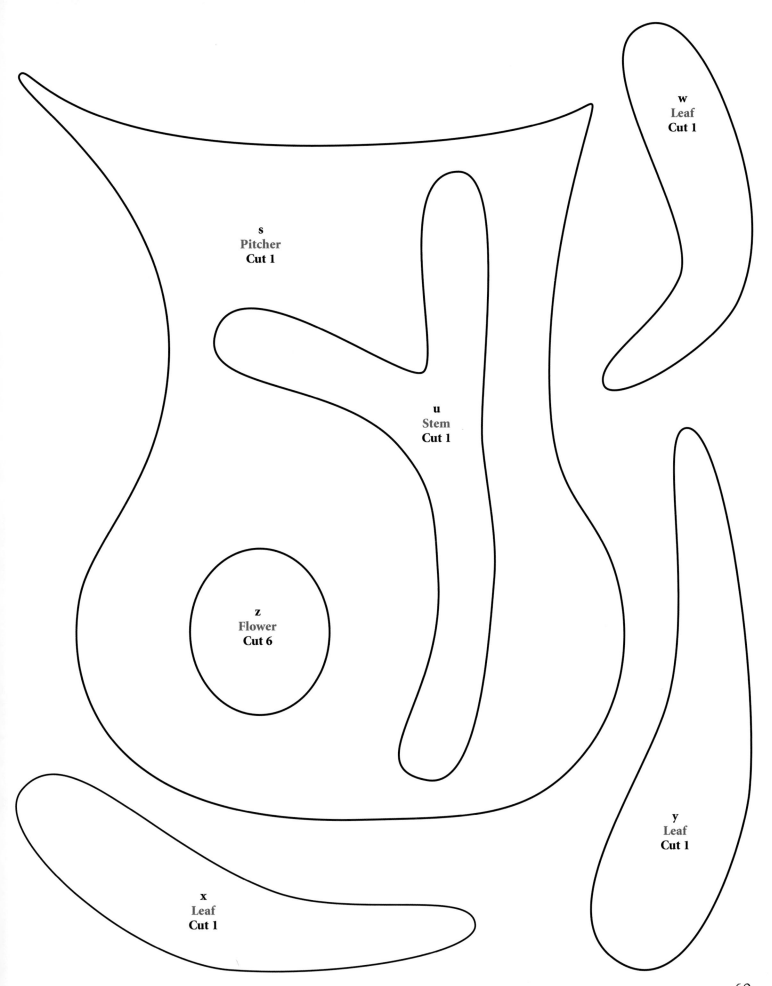

w
Leaf
Cut 1

s
Pitcher
Cut 1

u
Stem
Cut 1

z
Flower
Cut 6

y
Leaf
Cut 1

x
Leaf
Cut 1

Strawberries 'N' CREAM

When the days are warm enough to doff your coat and don your garden hat, it's time to pick strawberries! Cream fabrics give this sweet treat its old-fashioned elegance. And of course, it's made even better with appliqués — red berries, bell- and trumpet-shaped blooms, a vine-wrapped bee skep, and one happy little bluebird.

STRAWBERRIES 'N' CREAM
Finished Size: 60" x 71" (152 cm x 180 cm)

FABRIC REQUIREMENTS

$^3/_8$ yd (34 cm) of pink print No. 1

$^1/_2$ yd (46 cm) of pink print No. 2

18" x 22" (46 cm x 56 cm) piece of pink print No. 3

$^1/_4$ yd (23 cm) of pink print No. 4 for side border

$^1/_2$ yd (46 cm) of grey print No. 1

$^1/_4$ yd (23 cm) of grey print No. 2 for side border

18" x 22" (46 cm x 56 cm) piece of blue print No. 1

18" x 22" (46 cm x 56 cm) piece of blue print No. 2

$^1/_4$ yd (23 cm) of blue print No. 3 for side border

$^5/_8$ yd (57 cm) of yellow print No. 1

$^1/_2$ yd (46 cm) of yellow print No. 2

$^1/_4$ yd (23 cm) of yellow print No. 3 for side border

$1^1/_8$ yds (1.0 m) **total** of assorted pink, blue, yellow, and grey prints for sashings

$^1/_2$ yd (46 cm) **total** of assorted pink and blue prints for scalloped corners

$^3/_4$ yd (69 cm) **total** of assorted green prints

$^1/_4$ yd (23 cm) **total** of assorted yellow prints

$^1/_4$ yd (23 cm) **total** of assorted pink prints

$^1/_4$ yd (23 cm) **total** of assorted blue prints

$^1/_4$ yd (23 cm) **total** of assorted grey prints

$^1/_8$ yd (11 cm) **total** of assorted purple prints

$^1/_8$ yd (11 cm) **total** of assorted red prints

$^1/_2$ yd (46 cm) of binding fabric

4 yds (3.6 m) of backing fabric

72" x 90" batting

One $^5/_8$" dia. button

Green embroidery floss

CUTTING THE BACKGROUNDS AND BORDERS

*Yardage is based on 45"w fabric. Refer to **Rotary Cutting**, page 101, before beginning project. To help keep pieces organized, refer to photo and **Block Diagrams** to lay out the pieces as you cut.*

From pink print No. 1:
- Cut 2 background rectangles (No. 1 and No. 2) $9^1/_2$" x 14".

From grey print No. 1:
- Cut 1 background rectangle (No. 3) $40^1/_2$" x 14".

From yellow print No. 2:
- Cut 1 background rectangle (No. 4) $40^1/_2$" x 14".

From pink print No. 2:
- Cut 1 background rectangle (No. 5) 14" x $39^1/_2$".

From blue print No. 1:
- Cut 1 background rectangle (No. 6) $17^1/_2$" x $19^1/_2$".

From yellow print No. 1:
- Cut 1 background rectangle (No. 7) $17^1/_2$" x $21^1/_2$".

From pink print No. 3:
- Cut 1 background rectangle (No. 8) 14" x 20".

From blue print No. 2:
- Cut 1 background rectangle (No. 9) 14" x 20".

From pink print No. 4:
- Cut 1 border rectangle (No. 10) $5^1/_2$" x $34^1/_2$".

From blue print No. 3:
- Cut 1 border rectangle (No. 11) $5^1/_2$" x $36^1/_2$".

From yellow print No. 3:
- Cut 1 border rectangle (No. 12) $5^1/_2$" x $36^1/_2$".

From grey print No. 2:
- Cut 1 border rectangle (No. 13) $5^1/_2$" x $34^1/_2$".

From assorted pink, blue, yellow, and grey prints:
- Cut 4 sashing strips (Nos. 14-17) 14" x $2^1/_2$".
- Cut 1 sashing strip (No. 18) $17^1/_2$" x $3^1/_2$".
- Cut 2 sashing strips (No. 19 and No. 20) 3" x $21^1/_2$".
- Cut 2 sashing strips (No. 21 and No. 22) 3" x $22^1/_2$".

From binding fabric:
- Cut 6 strips $2^1/_2$"w.

CUTTING THE APPLIQUÉS

*Refer to **Making Templates**, page 104, to use patterns, page 77-83, to make templates. **Note:** Appliqué patterns provided do not include seam allowances. Measurements given for bias strips include a $^1/_4$" seam allowance. To help keep blocks organized, lay out all appliqué pieces with corresponding backgrounds as you cut.*

Blocks A and F

From assorted green prints:
- Cut 4 bias strips 1" x 23" for vines (A).
- Cut 8 stems; cut 8 in reverse (B).
- Cut 4 stems; cut 4 in reverse (C).
- Cut 8 large leaves (D).
- Cut 4 small leaves (E).
- Cut 8 strawberry leaves (F).
- Cut 8 strawberry caps (G).

From assorted red prints:
- Cut 8 strawberries (H).
- Cut 60 circles (I).
- Cut 4 flower centers (J).

From assorted pink, blue, yellow, grey, and purple prints:
- Cut 4 flowers (K).
- Cut 4 flower petals (L).
- Cut 4 flower bottoms (M).
- Cut 4 flower tops (N).
- Cut 8 scalloped corners on fold (O).

Block B

From assorted green prints:
- Cut 1 stem (P1, P2, P3, and P4).
- Cut 1 stem; cut 1 in reverse (Q).
- Cut 1 stem (R).
- Cut 1 each of flower caps (U and AA).
- Cut 1 flower cap; cut 1 in reverse (X).
- Cut 4 leaves (BB).

From assorted pink, blue, yellow, grey, and purple prints:
- Cut 1 flower (S).
- Cut 1 flower petal (T).
- Cut 1 flower; cut 1 in reverse (V).
- Cut 1 flower petal; cut 1 in reverse (W).
- Cut 1 flower (Y).
- Cut 1 flower petal (Z).

Block C

From yellow print No. 1:
- Cut 1 beehive on fold (CC).

From purple print:
- Cut 1 beehive opening (DD).

From assorted pink prints:
- Cut 1 ribbon (EE).
- Cut 1 flower (HH).
- Cut 1 leaf (OO).
- Cut 4 scalloped corners on fold (O).

From blue print:
- Cut 1 flower part (II).

From assorted red prints:
- Cut 1 flower center (JJ).
- Cut 1 strawberry (KK).
- Cut 12 circles (I).

From assorted green prints:
- Cut 1 ribbon (FF).
- Cut 2 leaves (GG).
- Cut 1 strawberry cap (LL).
- Cut 1 each of ribbons (MM and NN).

Block D

From assorted green prints:
- Cut 1 stem in reverse (P1, P2, P3, and P4).
- Cut 2 stems: cut 1 in reverse (PP).
- Cut 4 flower caps (TT).
- Cut 4 leaves (UU).

From assorted red, pink, blue, yellow, grey, and purple prints:
- Cut 4 flowers (QQ).
- Cut 4 flower petals (RR).
- Cut 4 flower centers (SS).

Block E

From assorted green prints:
- Cut 1 each of stems (VV and WW).
- Cut 1 vine (XX).
- Cut 6 leaves (g).

From assorted yellow, pink, blue, and purple prints:
- Cut 1 each of flower bottoms (YY, a, c, and e).
- Cut 1 each of flower tops (ZZ, b, d, and f).

From assorted red prints:
- Cut 24 circles (I).

From assorted blue prints:
- Cut 1 bird (h).
- Cut 1 bird wing (i).
- Cut 4 scalloped corners (O).

MAKING THE BLOCKS

*Refer to **Piecing and Pressing,** page 103, and **Needle-Turn Appliqué,** page 104, to assemble the blocks. Refer to **Block Diagrams** and **Quilt Top Diagram,** page 76, for placement. Working in alphabetical order, position pieces, then pin or baste in place on background rectangles before appliquéing.*

Blocks A and F

1. Sew the No. 1 and No. 3 background rectangles together to make **Block A** background.
2. Sew the No. 2 and No. 4 background rectangles together to make **Block F** background.
3. Appliqué the vines, stems, leaves, flower pieces, berries, and corners on backgrounds to make **Blocks A** and **F**.

Blocks A and F Diagram

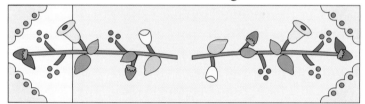

Unit 2

1. Appliqué the stems, leaves, and flower pieces on the No. 5 background rectangle to make Block B.
2. Sew No. 14 and No. 15 sashing strips to top and bottom of **Block B** to make **Unit 1**.
3. Sew No. 19 sashing strip to No. 21 sashing strip; then sew to right side of **Unit 1** to make **Unit 2**.

Unit 2

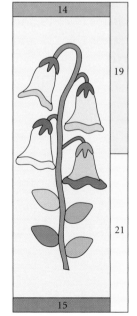

Units 3 and 4

1. Appliqué the beehive pieces, ribbons, leaves, flower pieces, berries, and corners on the No. 6 background rectangle. Sew button to strawberry cap.
2. Sew No. 18 sashing strip to bottom of **Block C** to make **Unit 3**.
3. Sew No. 20 sashing strip to No. 22 sashing strip to make **Unit 4**.

Unit 3   **Unit 4**

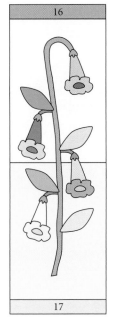

Unit 5

1. Sew No. 8 and No. 9 background rectangles together to make **Block D** background.
2. Appliqué the stems, leaves, and flower pieces on background to make **Block D**.
3. Sew the No. 16 and No. 17 sashing strips to **Block D** to make **Unit 5**.

Unit 5

Unit 6

1. Appliqué the vine, stems, leaves, flower pieces, berries, bird, and corners on the No. 7 background rectangle to make **Block E**. Stitch 4 stems with Stem Stitch using 3 strands of green embroidery floss.
2. Sew **Block E** to the bottom of **Unit 3** to make **Unit 6**.

Block E Diagram   **Unit 6**

ASSEMBLING THE QUILT TOP

*Referring to **Quilt Top Diagram**, page 76, and photo, page 72, for placement, sew the blocks together in the order listed below.*

1. Sew **Unit 2** to **Unit 6** to make **Unit 7**.
2. Sew **Unit 7** to **Unit 4** to make **Unit 8**.
3. Sew **Unit 8** to **Unit 5** to make **Unit 9**.
4. Sew **Blocks A** and **F** to the top and bottom of **Unit 9** to make **Unit 10**.
5. Sew No. 10 and No. 11 border rectangles together to make **Unit 11**.
6. Sew No. 12 and No. 13 border rectangles together to make **Unit 12**.
7. Sew **Units 11** and **12** to the sides of **Unit 10** to make quilt top.

FINISHING

1. Follow **Quilting**, page 106, to mark, layer, and quilt, as desired. Our quilt was machine quilted.
2. Follow **Making Straight Grain Binding**, page 110, to make $7^5/_8$ yds of $2^1/_2$"w binding.
3. Follow **Attaching Binding with Mitered Corners**, page 110, to bind quilt.

Blocks A and F

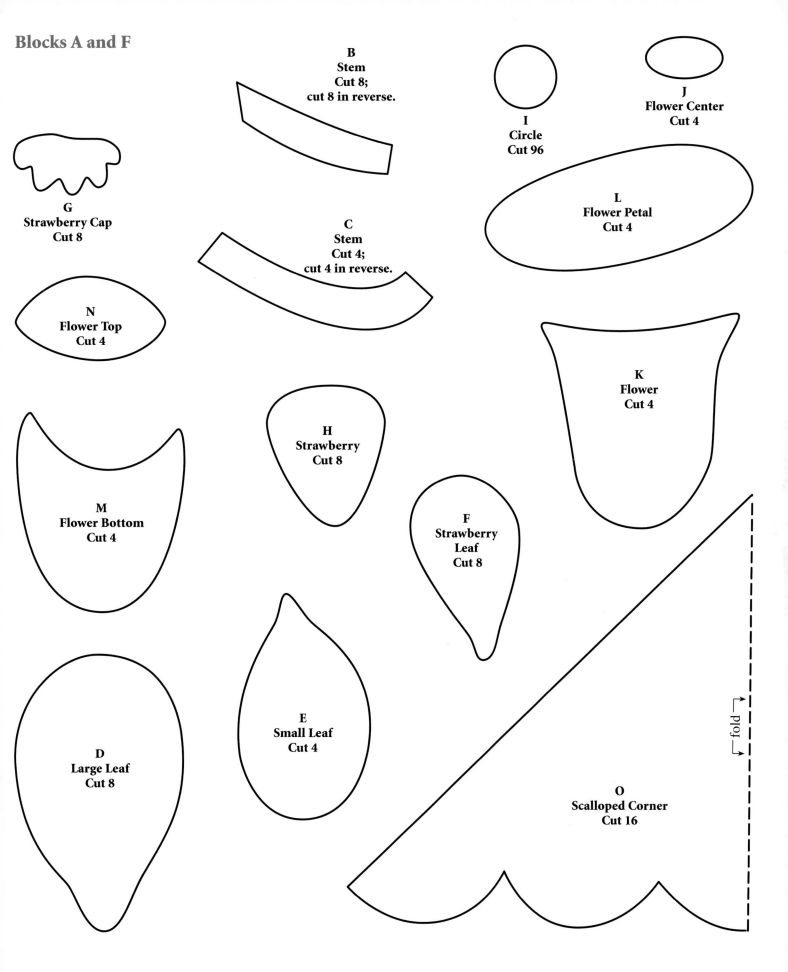

B
Stem
Cut 8;
cut 8 in reverse.

I
Circle
Cut 96

J
Flower Center
Cut 4

G
Strawberry Cap
Cut 8

C
Stem
Cut 4;
cut 4 in reverse.

L
Flower Petal
Cut 4

N
Flower Top
Cut 4

K
Flower
Cut 4

M
Flower Bottom
Cut 4

H
Strawberry
Cut 8

F
Strawberry
Leaf
Cut 8

D
Large Leaf
Cut 8

E
Small Leaf
Cut 4

fold

O
Scalloped Corner
Cut 16

NOTE: For patterns marked with a dashed fold line, match fold of pattern to fold of fabric and cut along solid lines.

Block B

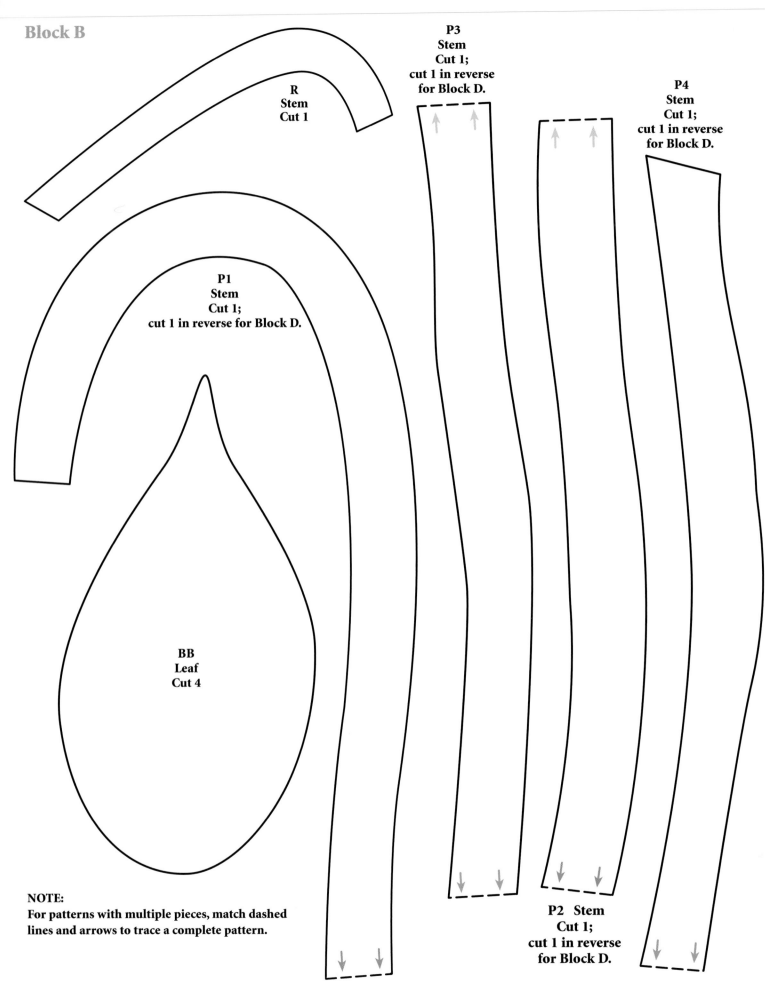

R
Stem
Cut 1

P3
Stem
Cut 1;
cut 1 in reverse
for Block D.

P4
Stem
Cut 1;
cut 1 in reverse
for Block D.

P1
Stem
Cut 1;
cut 1 in reverse for Block D.

BB
Leaf
Cut 4

P2   Stem
Cut 1;
cut 1 in reverse
for Block D.

NOTE:
For patterns with multiple pieces, match dashed
lines and arrows to trace a complete pattern.

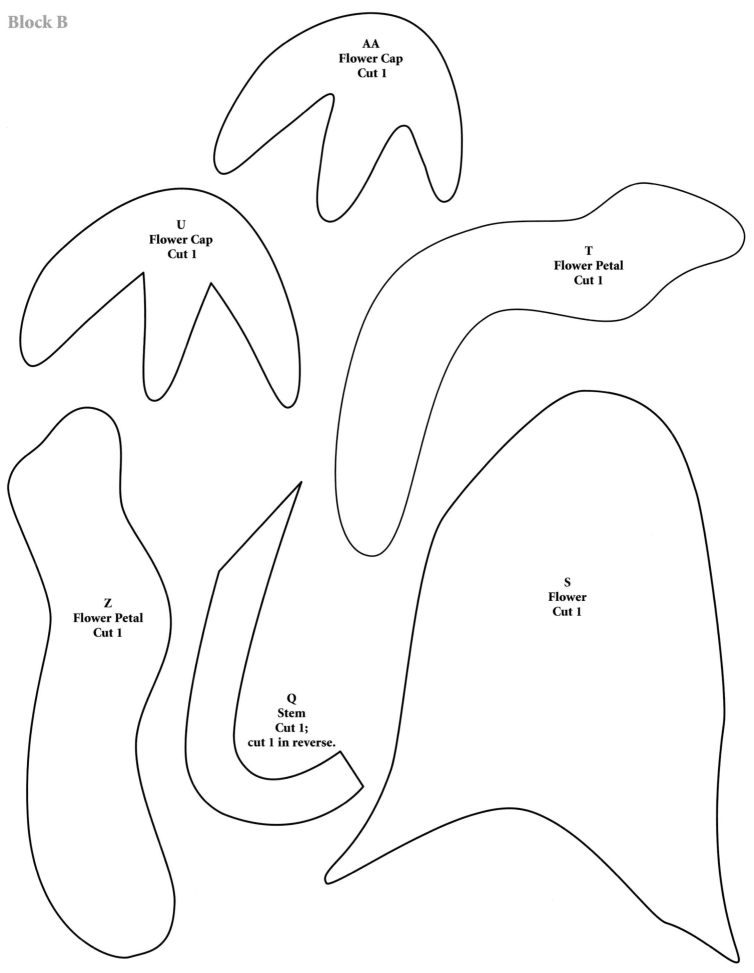

AA
Flower Cap
Cut 1

U
Flower Cap
Cut 1

T
Flower Petal
Cut 1

Z
Flower Petal
Cut 1

S
Flower
Cut 1

Q
Stem
Cut 1;
cut 1 in reverse.

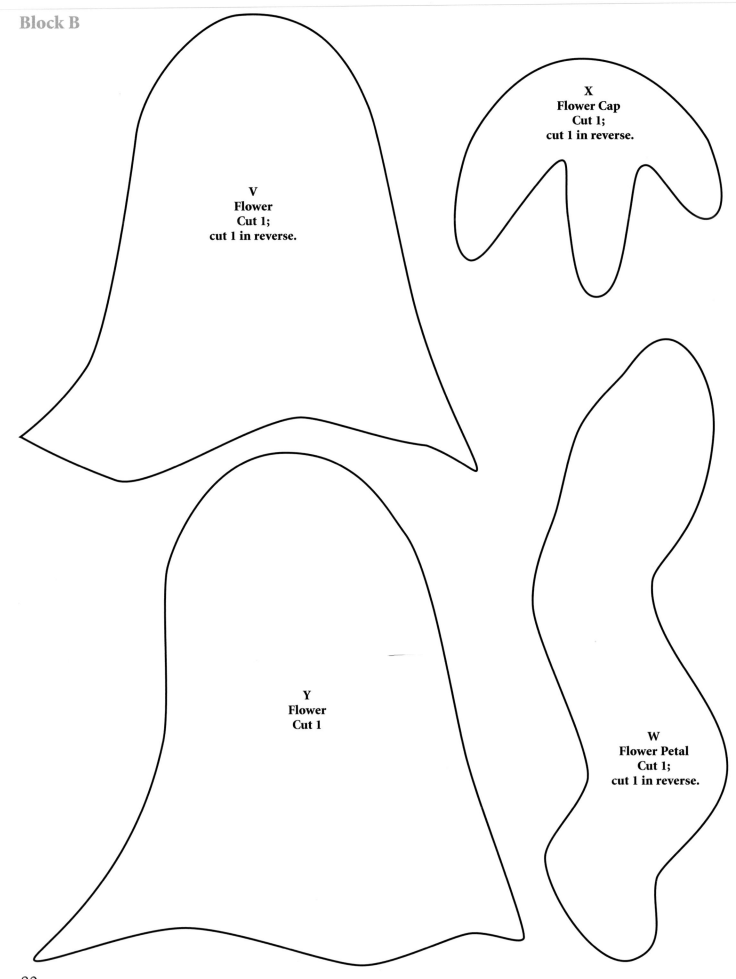

Block B

V
Flower
Cut 1;
cut 1 in reverse.

X
Flower Cap
Cut 1;
cut 1 in reverse.

Y
Flower
Cut 1

W
Flower Petal
Cut 1;
cut 1 in reverse.

Block C

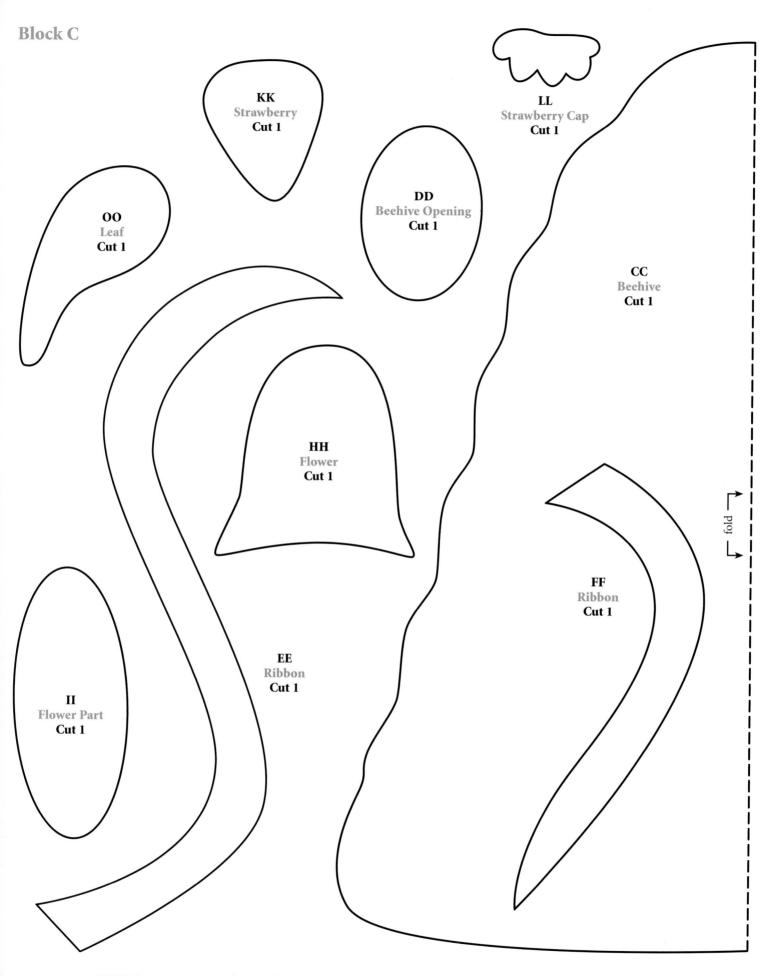

KK
Strawberry
Cut 1

LL
Strawberry Cap
Cut 1

OO
Leaf
Cut 1

DD
Beehive Opening
Cut 1

CC
Beehive
Cut 1

HH
Flower
Cut 1

fold

FF
Ribbon
Cut 1

EE
Ribbon
Cut 1

II
Flower Part
Cut 1

NOTE: For patterns marked with a dashed fold line, match fold of pattern to fold of fabric and cut along solid lines.

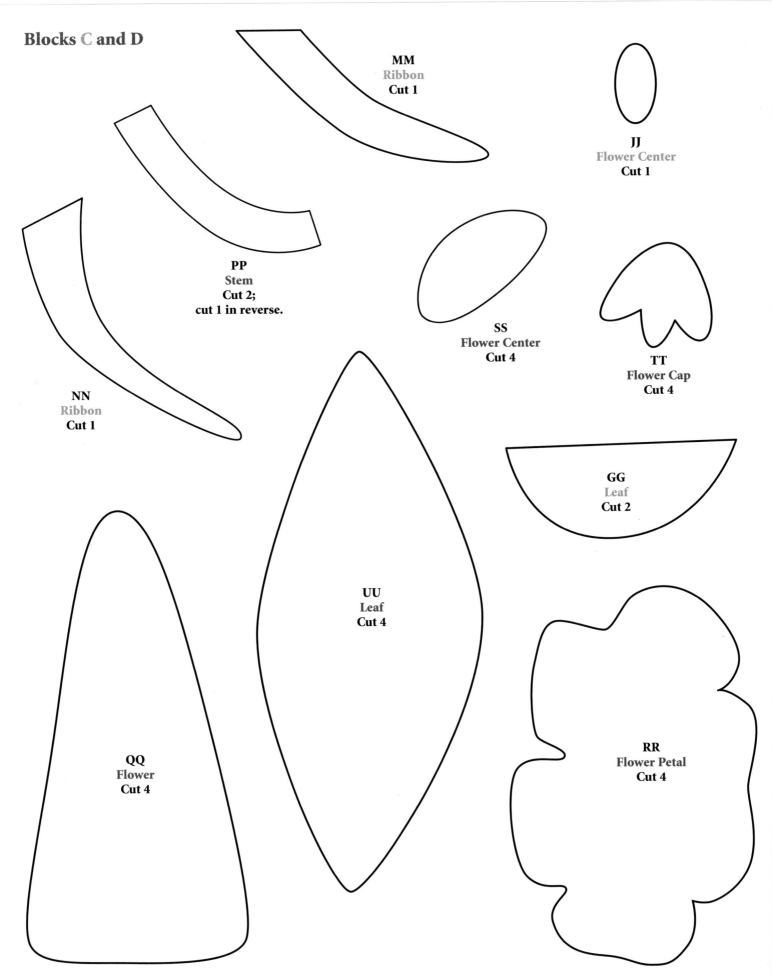

Blocks C and D

MM
Ribbon
Cut 1

JJ
Flower Center
Cut 1

PP
Stem
Cut 2;
cut 1 in reverse.

SS
Flower Center
Cut 4

TT
Flower Cap
Cut 4

NN
Ribbon
Cut 1

GG
Leaf
Cut 2

UU
Leaf
Cut 4

QQ
Flower
Cut 4

RR
Flower Petal
Cut 4

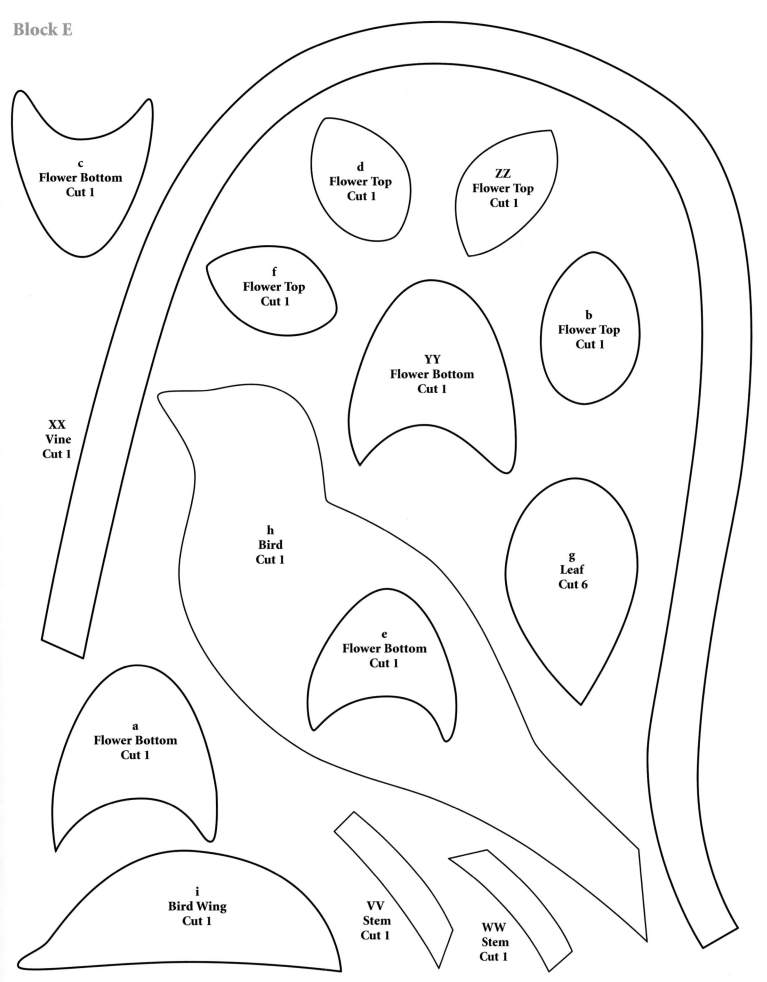

c
Flower Bottom
Cut 1

d
Flower Top
Cut 1

ZZ
Flower Top
Cut 1

f
Flower Top
Cut 1

b
Flower Top
Cut 1

YY
Flower Bottom
Cut 1

XX
Vine
Cut 1

h
Bird
Cut 1

g
Leaf
Cut 6

e
Flower Bottom
Cut 1

a
Flower Bottom
Cut 1

i
Bird Wing
Cut 1

VV
Stem
Cut 1

WW
Stem
Cut 1

Tulip SAMPLER

A snip of this, a scrap of that ... mix up your pastel fabrics and see what combinations work for you. Contrary to popular belief, stripes and checks get along just fine with floral prints. Once your quilt top is complete, consider quilting each block in a different manner from its neighbors. After all, the fun part of creating a quilt is in the discoveries you make along the way!

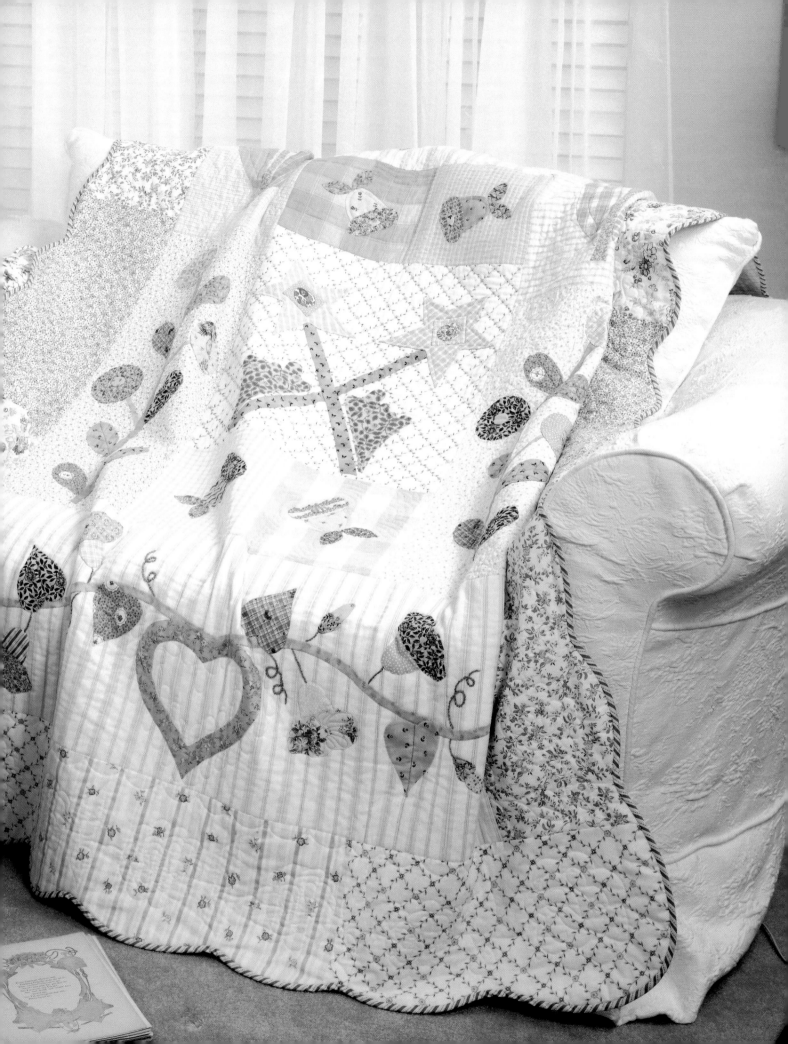

TULIP SAMPLER

Finished Size: 64" x 85" (163 cm x 216 cm)

FABRIC REQUIREMENTS

³/₈ yd (34 cm) of blue print No. 1 for borders

³/₈ yd (34 cm) of blue print No. 2 for borders

³/₈ yd (34 cm) of blue print No. 3 for borders

³/₈ yd (34 cm) of blue print No. 4 for borders

³/₈ yd (34 cm) of blue print No. 5 for background

³/₈ yd (34 cm) of green print No. 1 for borders

18" x 22" (46 cm x 56 cm) piece of green print No. 2 for background

18" x 22" (46 cm x 56 cm) piece of purple print for background

18" x 22" (46 cm x 56 cm) piece of yellow print No. 1 for background

⁵/₈ yd (57 cm) of yellow print No. 2 for background

18" x 22" (46 cm x 56 cm) piece of yellow print No. 3 for background

³/₈ yd (34 cm) of yellow print No. 4 for background

¹/₂ yd (46 cm) of yellow print No. 5 for background

³/₈ yd (34 cm) of pink print No. 1 for borders

³/₈ yd (34 cm) of pink print No. 2 for background

³/₈ yd (34 cm) of pink print No. 3 for background

³/₈ yd (34 cm) of pink print No. 4 for background

¹/₂ yd (46 cm) **each** of assorted pink, blue, yellow, green, and purple prints

³/₄ yd (69 cm) of binding fabric

5¹/₄ yds (4.8 m) of backing fabric

72" x 90" batting

Green embroidery floss

CUTTING THE BACKGROUNDS AND BORDERS

*Yardage is based on 45"w fabric. Refer to **Rotary Cutting**, page 101, before beginning project.*

From blue print No. 1:
- Cut 2 border rectangles (No. 1) $21^1/2$" x $10^1/2$".

From blue print No. 2:
- Cut 2 border rectangles (No. 2) $10^1/2$" x $21^1/2$".

From blue print No. 3:
- Cut 1 border rectangle (No. 3) $10^1/2$" x $22^1/2$".
- Cut 1 border rectangle (No. 4) $10^1/2$" x $21^1/2$".

From blue print No. 4:
- Cut 1 border rectangle (No. 5) $10^1/2$" x $21^1/2$".
- Cut 1 border rectangle (No. 6) $10^1/2$" x $22^1/2$".

From blue print No. 5:
- Cut 1 background rectangle (No. 9) $12^1/2$" x $22^1/2$".

From green print No. 1:
- Cut 2 border rectangles (No. 7) $21^1/2$" x $10^1/2$".

From green print No. 2:
- Cut 1 background rectangle (No. 13) 10" x 9".

From pink print No. 1:
- Cut 2 border rectangles (No. 8) $21^1/2$" x $10^1/2$".

From pink print No. 2:
- Cut 1 background rectangle (No. 10) $19^1/2$" x 11".

From pink print No. 3:
- Cut 1 background rectangle (No. 11) $12^1/2$" x $22^1/2$".

From pink print No. 4:
- Cut 1 background rectangle (No. 12) $12^1/2$" x $27^1/2$".

From yellow print No. 1:
- Cut 1 background rectangle (No. 14) 10" x 9".

From yellow print No. 2:
- Cut 1 background rectangle (No. 15) $19^1/2$" x $20^1/2$".

From yellow print No. 3:
- Cut 1 background rectangle (No. 16) 10" x $10^1/2$".

From yellow print No. 4:
- Cut 1 background rectangle (No. 17) $12^1/2$" x $27^1/2$".

From yellow print No. 5:
- Cut 1 background rectangle (No. 18) $43^1/2$" x $15^1/2$".

From purple print:
- Cut 1 background rectangle (No. 19) 10" x $10^1/2$".

From binding fabric:
- Cut 8 strips $2^1/2$"w.

CUTTING THE APPLIQUÉS

*Refer to **Making Templates**, page 104, to use patterns, pages 91-95, to make templates. **Note:** Appliqué patterns provided do not include seam allowances. Measurements given for bias strips and rectangles include $^1/4$" seam allowance. To help keep blocks organized, lay out all appliqué pieces with corresponding backgrounds as you cut.*

Block A

From assorted green prints:
- Cut 2 bias strips 1" x 23" for vines (A).
- Cut 4 flower caps (F).
- Cut 4 large leaves (G).
- Cut 2 small leaves (H).

From yellow print:
- Cut 4 flower centers (D).

From assorted pink and blue prints:
- Cut 4 flowers (B).
- Cut 4 flower petals (C).
- Cut 4 flower buds (E).
- Cut 1 heart on fold (I).

Block B

From assorted green prints:
- Cut 2 bias strips 1" x 24" for stems (J).
- Cut 2 bias strips $^3/4$" x 3" for small stems (K).
- Cut 2 bias strips $^3/4$" x 4" for small stems (L).
- Cut 6 leaves; cut 6 in reverse (O).

From assorted pink and blue prints:
- Cut 6 flowers (M).

From yellow print:
- Cut 6 flower centers (N).

Block C

From assorted green prints:
- Cut 8 leaves (S).

From assorted pink, blue, yellow, and purple prints:
- Cut 4 flowers (P).
- Cut 4 flower petals (Q).
- Cut 4 flower centers (R).

Block D

From assorted green prints:
- Cut 2 rectangles $1^1/2$" x 16" for stems (T).
- Cut 1 leaf; cut 1 in reverse (X).

From assorted pink, blue, and purple prints:
- Cut 2 flowers on fold (U).
- Cut 2 rectangles 2³/₈" x 2¹/₄" for flower centers (V).
- Cut 2 flower centers (W).

Block E

From assorted green prints:
- Cut 1 stem; cut 1 in reverse (Y1 and Y2).
- Cut 1 leaf; cut 1 in reverse (Z1 and Z2).
- Cut 1 leaf; cut 1 in reverse (AA).

From assorted pink and yellow prints:
- Cut 2 flowers (BB).

MAKING THE BLOCKS

*Refer to **Piecing and Pressing**, page 103, and **Needle-Turn Appliqué**, page 104, to assemble the blocks. Refer to **Block Diagrams** and **Quilt Top Diagram**, page 90, for placement. Working in alphabetical order, position pieces, then pin or baste in place on background rectangle before appliquéing.*

Block A

1. Appliqué vines, leaves, flower pieces, and heart on No. 18 background rectangle to make **Block A**.
2. Add stems and tendrils with Stem Stitch using 6 strands of green embroidery floss.

Block A Diagram

Block B

1. Appliqué stems, leaves, and flower pieces on No. 12 and No. 17 background rectangles to make **Block B**. Make 1 **Block B**; make 1 **Block B** in reverse.

Block B Diagram

Block C

1. Appliqué leaves and flower pieces on Nos. 13, 14, 16, and 19 background rectangles. Make 2 **Block C's**; make 2 **Block C's** in reverse.

Block C Diagram

Block D

Appliqué stems, leaves, and flower pieces on No. 15 background rectangle to make **Block D**.

Block D Diagram

ASSEMBLING THE QUILT TOP

*Referring to **Quilt Top Diagram**, page 90, and photo, page 86, for placement, sew the blocks together in the order listed below.*

1. Sew 1 **Block C** to 1 reverse **Block C** to make **Unit 1**. Make 2 **Unit 1's**.

Unit 1 (make 2)

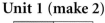

2. Sew a **Unit 1** to the top and bottom of **Block D** to make **Unit 2**.

Unit 2

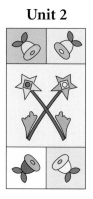

3. Sew a No. 10 background rectangle to the top of **Unit 2** to make **Unit 3**.

Unit 3

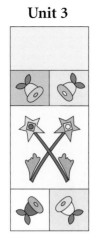

4. Sew a **Block B** to a No. 9 background rectangle to make **Unit 4** and a reverse **Block B** to a No. 11 background rectangle to make **Unit 5**.

Unit 4   Unit 5

5. Sew **Unit 3**, **Unit 4**, and **Unit 5** together to make **Unit 6**.

Unit 6

6. Refer to **Block E Diagram** and photo, page 86, for placement. Appliqué stems, leaves, and flowers on **Unit 6**.

Block E Diagram

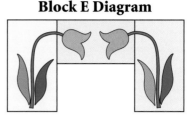

7. Sew **Block A** to the bottom of **Unit 6** to make quilt top center.

ADDING THE BORDERS

*Referring to **Quilt Top Diagram**, page 90, for placement, sew the border rectangles together in the order listed below.*

1. Sew border rectangles Nos. 2, 3, and 5 together to make left side border.

2. Sew border rectangles Nos. 6, 4, and 2 together to make right side border.

3. Sew border rectangles Nos. 1, 7, and 8 together to make top border.

4. Sew border rectangles Nos. 8, 7, and 1 together to make bottom border.

5. Sew side borders, then top and bottom borders to quilt top center.

6. Refer to **Making Templates**, page 104, and use Side Scallop and Corner Scallop patterns to make the templates for the scalloped border.

7. Trace the scalloped border onto quilt top. **Note:** If you will be machine quilting, do not cut out scalloped border until quilting has been completed.

FINISHING

1. Follow **Quilting**, page 106, to mark, layer, and quilt as desired. Our quilt was machine quilted.

2. Cut out scalloped border. Sew binding strips together to make a continuous bias binding strip. Follow Steps 1 and 2 of **Attaching Binding with Mitered Corners**, page 110, to pin binding to front of quilt. Sew binding to quilt, easing curves and leaving a 2" overlap. Trim off excess binding and stitch overlap in place. Fold binding over to quilt backing and pin in place, covering stitching line. Blind stitch binding to backing.

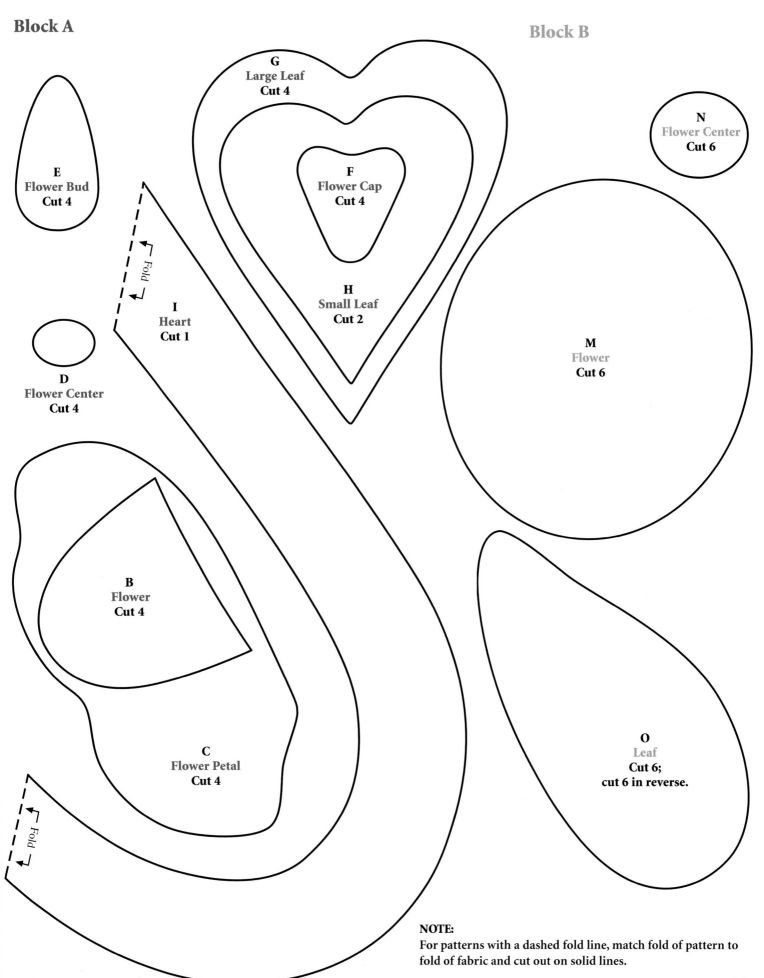

Block A

Block B

E
Flower Bud
Cut 4

G
Large Leaf
Cut 4

F
Flower Cap
Cut 4

N
Flower Center
Cut 6

Fold

I
Heart
Cut 1

H
Small Leaf
Cut 2

M
Flower
Cut 6

D
Flower Center
Cut 4

B
Flower
Cut 4

O
Leaf
Cut 6;
cut 6 in reverse.

C
Flower Petal
Cut 4

Fold

NOTE:
For patterns with a dashed fold line, match fold of pattern to fold of fabric and cut out on solid lines.

91

Blocks C, D, and E

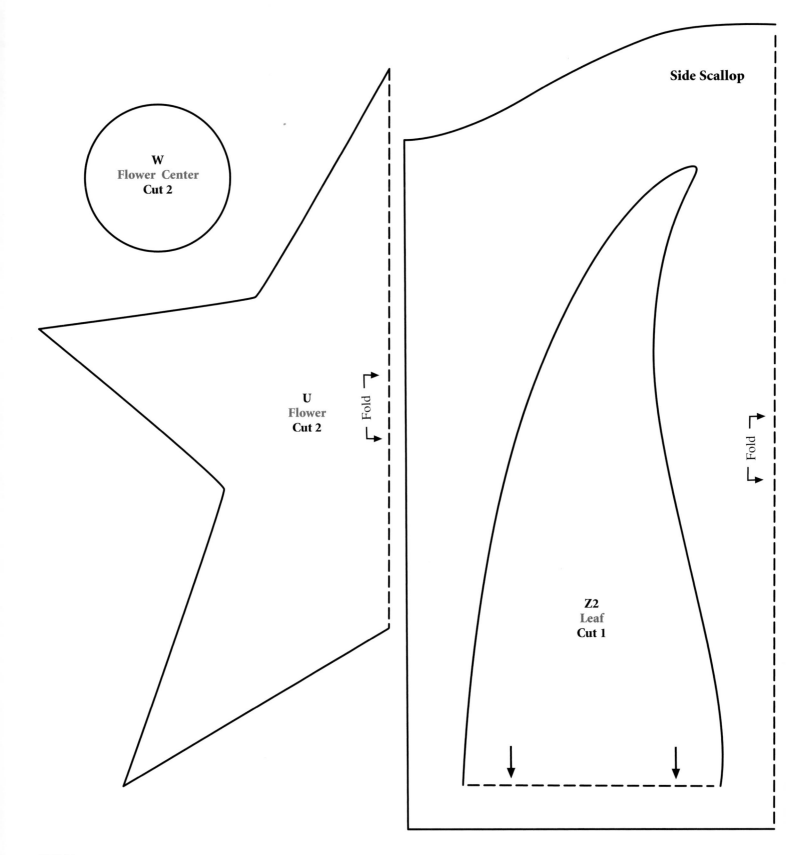

W
Flower Center
Cut 2

Side Scallop

U
Flower
Cut 2

Fold

Fold

Z2
Leaf
Cut 1

NOTE:
For patterns with multiple pieces (e.g. pattern pieces labeled A1 and A2), match dashed lines and arrows to trace a complete pattern. For patterns with a dashed fold line, match fold of pattern to fold of fabric and cut out on solid lines.

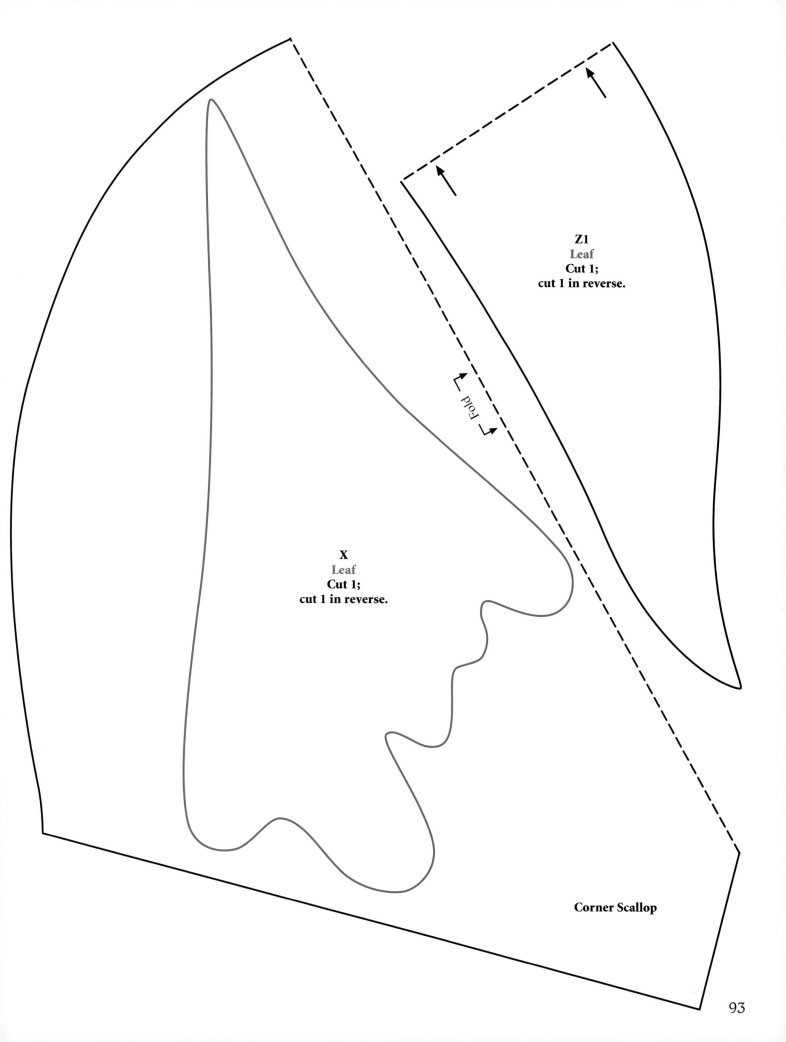

Z1
Leaf
**Cut 1;
cut 1 in reverse.**

Fold

X
Leaf
**Cut 1;
cut 1 in reverse.**

Corner Scallop

93

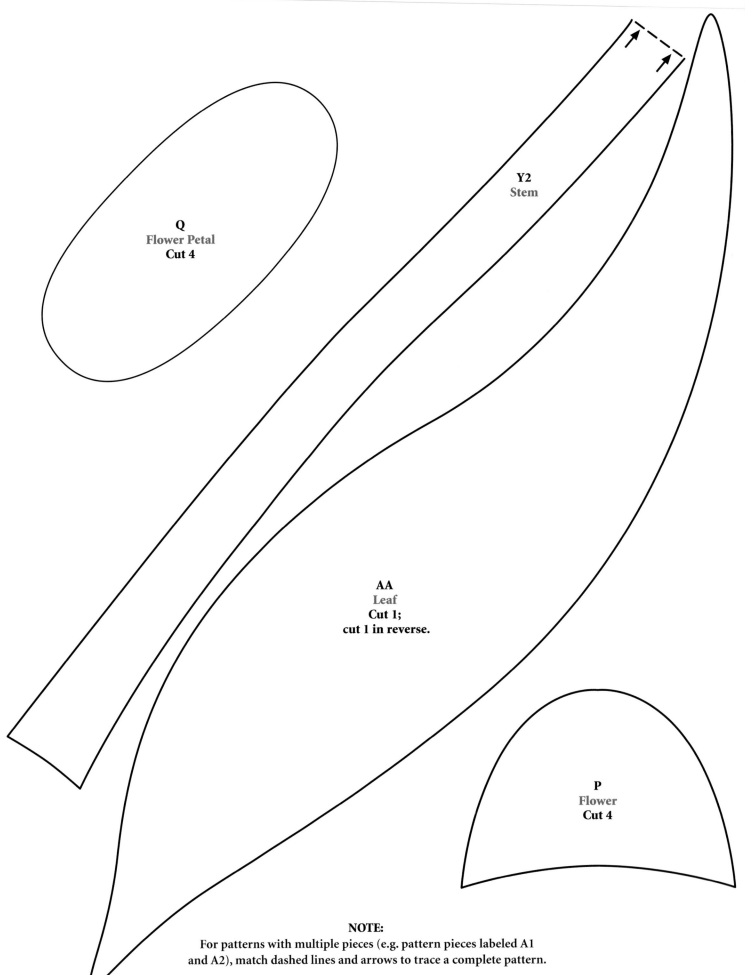

Q
Flower Petal
Cut 4

Y2
Stem

AA
Leaf
**Cut 1;
cut 1 in reverse.**

P
Flower
Cut 4

NOTE:
For patterns with multiple pieces (e.g. pattern pieces labeled A1
and A2), match dashed lines and arrows to trace a complete pattern.

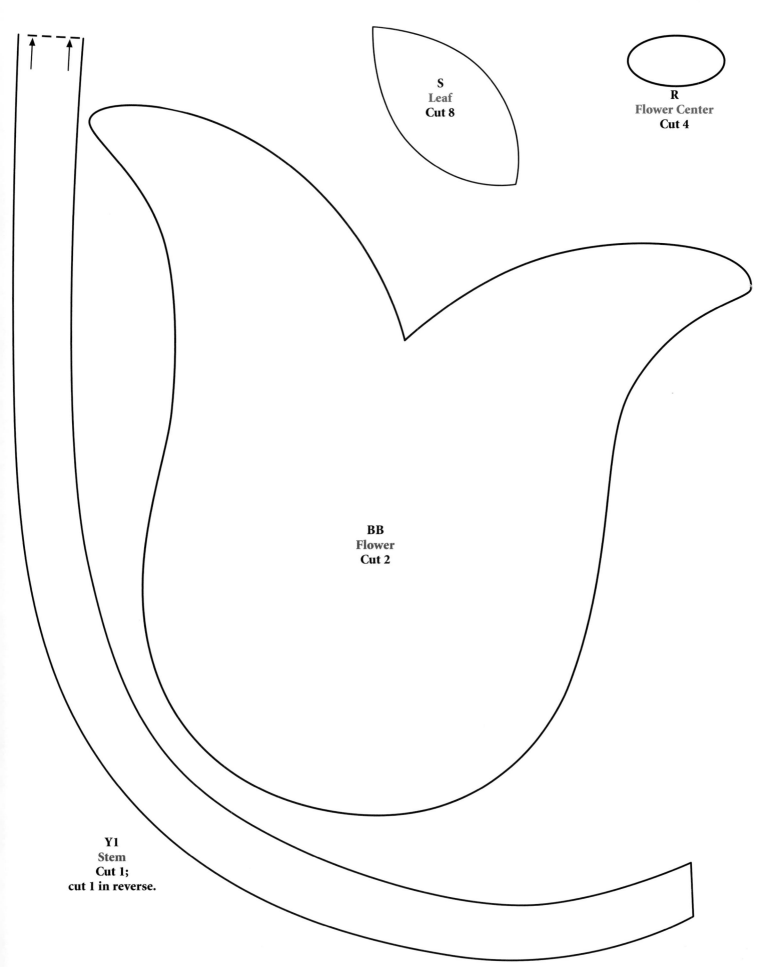

S
Leaf
Cut 8

R
Flower Center
Cut 4

BB
Flower
Cut 2

Y1
Stem
Cut 1;
cut 1 in reverse.

95

Summer SQUARES

Viewing this little quilt is like looking through a multi-paned window to see a riotous summer garden in bloom. Or perhaps it's an aerial view of nine colorful garden plots. Either way, the strippy blocks and morning glory border are the perfect showcase for your vintage fabric scraps.

SUMMER SQUARES

Block Size: 12" x 12" (31 x 31 cm)
Finished Size: 53" x 53" (135 cm x 135cm)

FABRIC REQUIREMENTS

$1^1/2$ yds (1.4 m) **total** of pink, blue, and green dot prints for borders

$1/8$ yd (11 cm) **total** of assorted white prints

$3^1/2$ yds (3.2 m) **total** of assorted pink, blue, and yellow prints

$1^5/8$ yds (1.5 m) **total** of assorted green prints

$1/2$ yd (46 cm) of binding fabric

$3^1/2$ yds (3.2 m) of backing fabric

72" x 90" batting

CUTTING THE BLOCKS AND BORDERS

*Yardage is based on 45"w fabric. Refer to **Rotary Cutting**, page 101, and **Adding Squared Borders**, page 105, before beginning project.*

From pink, blue, and green dot prints:
- Cut 2 top and bottom borders $36^1/2$" x $8^1/2$".
- Cut 2 side borders $8^1/2$" x $52^1/2$".

From assorted white prints:
- Cut 9 squares (No. 1) $3^1/2$" x $3^1/2$".

From assorted pink, blue, and yellow prints:
- Cut 18 rectangles (No. 2) 2" x $3^1/2$".
- Cut 36 rectangles (No. 3) 2" x $6^1/2$".
- Cut 36 rectangles (No. 4) 2" x $9^1/2$".
- Cut 18 rectangles (No. 5) 2" x $12^1/2$".

From assorted binding fabrics:
- Cut 6 strips $2^1/2$" w.

CUTTING THE APPLIQUÉS

*Refer to **Making Templates**, page 104, to use patterns, page 99, to make templates. **Note:** Appliqué patterns provided do not include seam allowances. Measurements given for bias strips include $1/4$" seam allowance.*

From assorted green prints:
- Cut 2 bias strips 1" x 28" for vines (A).
- Cut 2 bias strips 1" x 31" for vines (B).
- Cut 8 small leaves (C).
- Cut 6 large leaves (D).
- Cut 10 flower caps (F).
- Cut 9 flower bud caps (J).

From assorted pink and blue prints:
- Cut 10 flower bases (E).
- Cut 10 flower petals (G).

From assorted yellow prints:
- Cut 10 flower centers (H).

From assorted pink, blue, and yellow prints:
- Cut 9 flower buds (I).

MAKING THE BLOCKS

Refer to **Piecing and Pressing**, page 103, and **Block Assembly Diagram**, page 100, to piece the No. 1 square and the Nos. 2-5 strips together as shown. Use 4 different fabrics for each block as shown. Make 9 blocks.

Block Assembly Diagram

ASSEMBLING THE QUILT TOP

1. Refer to **Quilt Top Diagram**, page 100, and photo to sew the 9 blocks together to form quilt top center.
2. Refer to **Adding Squared Borders**, page 105, to sew the top and bottom borders, then the side borders to quilt top center.
3. Refer to **Needle-Turn Appliqué**, page 104, for techniques. Refer to **Quilt Top Diagram**, page 100, and photo for placement. Working in alphabetical order, position vines, leaves, and flower pieces on borders, then pin or baste in place and appliqué.

FINISHING

1. Follow **Quilting**, page 106, to mark, layer, and quilt as desired. Our quilt was machine quilted.
2. Follow **Making Straight Grain Binding**, page 110, to make 6 1/4 yds of 2 1/2"w binding.
3. Follow **Attaching Binding with Mitered Corners**, page 110, to bind quilt.

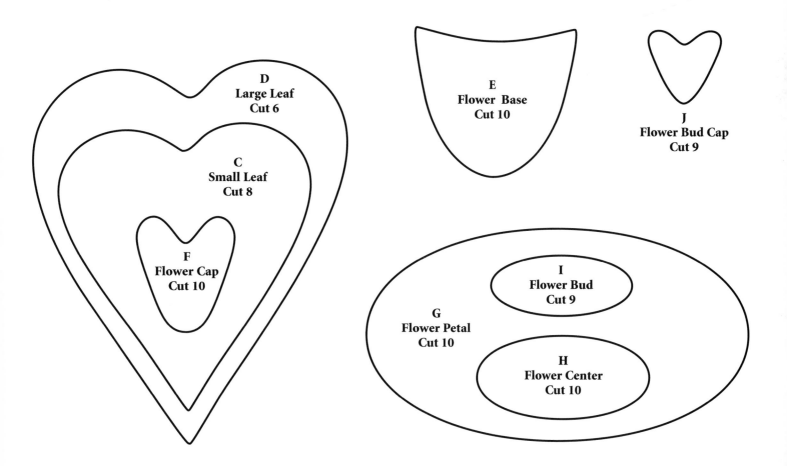

D Large Leaf Cut 6

C Small Leaf Cut 8

F Flower Cap Cut 10

E Flower Base Cut 10

J Flower Bud Cap Cut 9

G Flower Petal Cut 10

I Flower Bud Cut 9

H Flower Center Cut 10

GENERAL INSTRUCTIONS

Complete instructions are given for making each of the quilts shown in this book. To make your quilting easier and more enjoyable, we encourage you to carefully read all of the general instructions, study the color photographs, and familiarize yourself with the individual project instructions before beginning a project.

FABRICS

Selecting Fabrics

Choose high-quality, medium-weight 100% cotton fabrics such as broadcloth or calico. All-cotton fabrics hold a crease better, fray less, and are easier to quilt than cotton/polyester blends. All the fabrics for a quilt should be of comparable weight and weave. Check the end of the fabric bolt for fiber content and width.

The yardage requirements listed for each project are based on 45" wide fabric with a "usable" width of 42" after shrinkage and trimming selvages. Your actual usable width will probably vary slightly from fabric to fabric. Though most fabrics will yield 42" or more, if you find a fabric that you suspect will yield a narrower usable width, you will need to purchase additional yardage to compensate. Our recommended yardage lengths should be adequate for occasional re-squaring of fabric when many cuts are required, but it never hurts to buy a little more fabric for insurance against a narrower usable width, the occasional cutting error, or to have on hand for making coordinating projects.

Preparing Fabrics

All fabrics should be washed, dried, and pressed before cutting.

1. To check colorfastness before washing, cut a small piece of the fabric and place in a glass of hot water with a little detergent. Leave fabric in the water for a few minutes. Remove fabric from water and blot with white paper towels. If any color bleeds onto the towels, wash the fabric separately with warm water and detergent, then rinse until the water runs clear. If fabric continues to bleed, choose another fabric.

2. Unfold yardage and separate fabrics by color. To help reduce raveling, use scissors to snip a small triangle from each corner of your fabric pieces. Machine wash fabrics in warm water with a small amount of mild laundry detergent. Do not use fabric softener. Rinse well and then dry fabrics in the dryer, checking long fabric lengths occasionally to make sure they are not tangling.

3. To make ironing easier, remove fabrics from dryer while they are slightly damp. Refold each fabric lengthwise (as it was on the bolt) with wrong sides together and matching selvages. If necessary, adjust slightly at selvages so that fold lays flat. Press each fabric using a steam iron set on "Cotton."

ROTARY CUTTING

Based on the idea that you can easily cut strips of fabric and then cut those strips into smaller pieces, rotary cutting has brought speed and accuracy to quiltmaking. Observe safety precautions when using the rotary cutter, since it is extremely sharp. Develop a habit of retracting the blade guard just before making a cut and closing it immediately afterward, before laying down the cutter.

1. Follow **Preparing Fabrics** to wash, dry, and press fabrics.

2. Cut all strips from the selvage-to-selvage width of the fabric unless otherwise indicated in project instructions. Place fabric on the cutting mat, as shown in **Fig. 1**, with the fold of the fabric toward you. To straighten the uneven fabric edge, make the first "squaring up" cut by placing the right edge of the rotary cutting ruler over the left raw edge of the fabric. Place right-angle triangle (or another rotary cutting ruler) with the lower edge carefully aligned with the fold and the left edge against the ruler (**Fig. 1**). Hold the ruler firmly with your left hand, placing your little finger off the left edge of the ruler to anchor it. Remove the triangle, pick up the rotary cutter, and retract the blade guard. Using a smooth, downward motion, make the cut by running the blade of the rotary cutter firmly along the right edge of the ruler (**Fig. 2**). Always cut in a direction away from your body and immediately close the blade guard after each cut.

Fig. 1   **Fig. 2**

3. To cut each of the strips required for a project, place the ruler over the cut edge of the fabric, aligning desired marking on the ruler with the cut edge (**Fig. 3**); make the cut. When cutting several strips from a single piece of fabric, it is important to occasionally use the ruler and triangle to ensure that cuts are still at a perfect right angle to the fold. If not, repeat Step 2 to straighten.

Fig. 3

4. To square up selvage ends of a strip before cutting pieces, refer to Fig. 4 and place folded strip on mat with selvage ends to your right. Aligning a horizontal marking on ruler with 1 long edge of strip, use rotary cutter to trim selvage to make end of strip square and even (**Fig. 4**). Turn strip (or entire mat) so that cut end is to your left before making subsequent cuts.

Fig. 4

5. Pieces such as rectangles and squares can now be cut from strips. Usually strips remain folded, and pieces are cut in pairs after ends of strips are squared up. To cut squares or rectangles from a strip, place ruler over left end of strip, aligning desired marking on ruler with cut end of strip. To ensure perfectly square cuts, align a horizontal marking on ruler with 1 long edge of strip (**Fig. 5**) before making the cut.

Fig. 5

6. To cut 2 triangles from a square, cut square the size indicated in the project instructions. Cut square once diagonally to make 2 triangles (**Fig. 6**).

Fig. 6

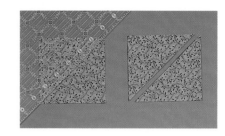

7. To cut 4 triangles from a square, cut square the size indicated in the project instructions. Cut square twice diagonally to make 4 triangles (**Fig. 7**). You may find it helpful to use a small rotary cutting mat so that the mat can be turned to make second cut without disturbing fabric pieces.

Fig. 7

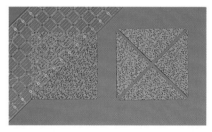

8. After some practice, you may want to try stacking up to 6 fabric layers when making cuts. When stacking strips, match long cut edges and follow Step 4 to square up ends of strip stack. Carefully turn stack (or entire mat) so that squared-up ends are to your left before making subsequent cuts. After cutting, check accuracy of pieces. Some shapes, such as diamonds, are more difficult to cut accurately in stacks.

9. In some cases, strips will be sewn together into strip sets before being cut into smaller units. When cutting a strip set, align a seam in strip set with a horizontal marking on the ruler to maintain square cuts (**Fig. 8**). We do not recommend stacking strip sets for rotary cutting.

Fig. 8

10. Most borders for quilts in this book are cut along the more stable lengthwise grain to minimize wavy edges caused by stretching. To remove selvages before cutting lengthwise strips, place fabric on mat with selvages to your left and squared-up end at bottom of mat. Placing ruler over selvage and using squared-up edge instead of fold, follow Step 2 to cut away selvages as you did raw edges (**Fig. 9**). After making a cut the length of the mat, move the next section of fabric to be cut onto the mat. Repeat until you have removed selvages from required length of fabric.

Fig. 9

11. After removing selvages, place ruler over left edge of fabric, aligning desired marking on ruler with cut edge of fabric. Make cuts as in Step 3. After each cut, move next section of fabric onto mat as in Step 10.

PIECING AND PRESSING

Precise cutting, followed by accurate piecing and careful pressing, will ensure that all the pieces of your quilt top fit together well.

Piecing

Set sewing machine stitch length for approximately 11 stitches per inch. Use a new, sharp needle suited for medium-weight woven fabric.

Use a neutral-colored general-purpose sewing thread (not quilting thread) in the needle and in the bobbin. Stitch first on a scrap of fabric to check upper and bobbin thread tension; make any adjustments necessary.

For good results, it is essential that you stitch with an accurate $1/4$" seam allowance. On many sewing machines, the measurement from the needle to the outer edge of the presser foot is $1/4$". If this is the case with your machine, the presser foot is your best guide. If not, measure $1/4$" from the needle and mark throat plate with a piece of masking tape. Special presser feet that are exactly $1/4$" wide are also available for most sewing machines.

When piecing, always place pieces right sides together and match raw edges; pin if necessary. (If using straight pins, remove the pins just before they reach the sewing machine needle.)

Chain Piecing

Chain piecing whenever possible will make your work go faster and will usually result in more accurate piecing. Stack the pieces you will be sewing beside your machine in the order you will need them and in a position that will allow you to easily pick them up. Pick up each pair of pieces, carefully place them together as they will be sewn, and feed them into the machine one after the other. Stop between each pair only long enough to pick up the next and don't cut thread between pairs (**Fig. 10**). After all pieces are sewn, cut threads, press, and go on to the next step, again chain piecing when possible.

Fig. 10

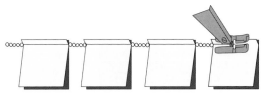

Sewing Across Seam Intersections

When sewing across the intersection of 2 seams, place pieces right sides together and match seams exactly, making sure seam allowances are pressed in opposite directions (**Fig. 11**). To prevent fabric from shifting, you may wish to pin in place.

Fig. 11

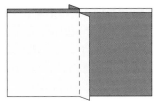

Sewing Bias Seams

Care should be used in handling and stitching bias edges since they stretch easily. After sewing the seam, carefully press seam allowance to 1 side, making sure not to stretch fabric.

Sewing Sharp Points

To ensure sharp points when joining triangular or diagonal pieces, stitch across the center of the "X" (shown in pink) formed on the wrong side by previous seams (**Fig. 12**).

Fig. 12

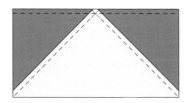

Trimming Seam Allowances

When sewing with triangle pieces, some seam allowances may extend beyond the edges of the sewn pieces. Trim away "dog ears" that extend beyond the edges of the sewn pieces (**Fig. 13**).

Fig. 13

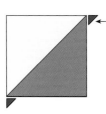

Pressing

Use a steam iron set on "Cotton" for all pressing. Press as you sew, taking care to prevent small folds along seamlines. Seam allowances are almost always pressed to one side, usually toward the darker fabric. However, to reduce bulk it may occasionally be necessary to press seam allowances toward the lighter fabric or even to press them open. In order to prevent a dark fabric seam allowance from showing through a light fabric, trim the darker seam allowance slightly narrower than the lighter seam allowance. To press long seams, such as those in long strip sets, without curving or other distortion, lay strips across the width of the ironing board.

APPLIQUÉ
Making Templates

Patterns for piecing templates include seam allowances; those for appliqué do not. To make a template from a pattern, use a permanent fine-point marker or pen to carefully trace the pattern onto template plastic, making sure to label the template and to transfer any alignment or grain line markings. Some patterns have multiple pieces (e.g., pattern pieces labeled A1 and A2). Match dashed lines and arrows to trace a complete pattern. Cut out template along drawn line. Check your template against the original pattern for accuracy.

Needle-Turn Appliqué

In this traditional hand appliqué method, the needle is used to turn the seam allowance under as you sew the appliqué to the background fabric using a Blind Stitch. When stitching, match the color of thread to the color of appliqué to disguise your stitches. Appliqué each piece starting with the ones directly on the background fabric. It is not necessary to appliqué areas that will be covered by another appliqué. Stitches on the right side of fabric should not show. Stitches on the edge of an appliqué and on background fabric should be equal in length. Clipped areas should be secured with a few extra stitches to prevent fraying.

1. Place template on right side of appliqué fabric. Use a pencil to lightly draw around template, leaving at least $1/2$" between shapes; repeat for number of shapes specified in project instructions.
2. Cut out shapes approximately $3/16$" outside drawn line. Clip inside curves and points up to, but not through, drawn line. Arrange shapes on background fabric and pin or baste in place.
3. Thread a sharps needle with a single strand of general-purpose sewing thread; knot one end.
4. Pin center of appliqué to right side of background fabric. Begin on as straight an edge as possible and use point of needle to turn under a small amount of seam allowance, concealing drawn line on appliqué. Hold seam allowance in place with thumb of your non-sewing hand (**Fig. 14**).

Fig. 14

Fig. 18   **Fig. 19**

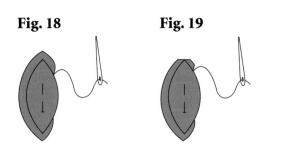

5. To stitch, bring needle up through background fabric at 1, even with turned edge of appliqué (**Fig. 15**).

Fig. 15

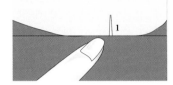

6. Insert needle into turned edge at 2, directly across from 1. Bring needle out of folded edge at 3 (**Fig. 16**). Insert needle into background fabric at 4, even with edge of appliqué and directly across from 3. Bring needle up through background fabric at 5, forming a small stitch on wrong side of fabric (**Fig. 17**).

Fig. 16   **Fig. 17**

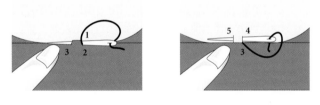

7. Continue needle-turning method to completely secure appliqué, referring to information below about stitching outward points and bias strips.

Stitching Outward Points: Appliqué long edge of shape until you are about ¹/₂" from the point (**Fig. 18**). Turn seam allowance under at point (**Fig. 19**). Turn remainder of seam allowance between stitching and point, using non-stitching thumb to hold allowance in place. Stitch to point, taking 2 or 3 stitches at top of point to secure. Turn under small amount of seam allowance past point and resume stitching.

Stitching Pressed Bias Strips: Since seam allowances have already been stitched or pressed under during preparation of bias strips used as appliqués, simply baste bias strip to background fabric, then stitch in place along edges using the same blind stitch used in needle-turning.

BORDERS

Borders cut along the lengthwise grain will lie flatter than borders cut along the crosswise grain. Cutting lengths given for borders in this book are exact. You may wish to add an extra 2" of length at each end for "insurance"; borders will be trimmed after measuring completed center section of quilt top.

Adding Squared Borders

1. Mark the center of each edge of quilt top.
2. Most of the borders in this book have the side borders added first. To add side borders, measure across center of quilt top to determine length of borders (**Fig. 20**). Trim side borders to the determined length.

Fig. 20

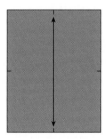

3. Mark center of 1 long edge of side border. Matching center marks and raw edges, pin border to quilt top, easing in any fullness; stitch. Repeat for other side border.

4. Measure center of quilt top, including attached borders, to determine length of top and bottom borders. Trim top and bottom borders to the determined length. Repeat Step 3 to add borders to quilt top (**Fig. 21**).

Fig. 21

QUILTING

Quilting holds the 3 layers (top, batting, and backing) of the quilt together and can be done by hand or machine. Our project instructions tell you which method is used on each project. Because marking, layering, and quilting are interrelated and may be done in different orders depending on circumstances, please read the entire **Quilting** *section, pages 106 - 109, before beginning the quilting process on your project.*

Types Of Quilting
In the Ditch Quilting

Quilting very close to a seamline or appliqué is called "in the ditch" quilting. This type of quilting does not need to be marked. When quilting in the ditch, quilt on the side **opposite** the seam allowance.

Outline Quilting

Quilting approximately ¹/₄" from a seam or appliqué is called "outline" quilting. Outline quilting may be marked, or you may place ¹/₄"w masking tape along seamlines and quilt along the opposite edge of the tape. (Do not leave tape on quilt longer than necessary, since it may leave an adhesive residue.)

Ornamental Quilting

Quilting decorative lines or designs is called "ornamental" quilting (**Fig. 22**). This type of quilting should be marked before you baste quilt layers together.

Fig. 22

Marking Quilting Lines

Fabric marking pencils, various types of chalk markers, and fabric marking pens with inks that disappear with exposure to air or water are readily available and work well for different applications. Lead pencils work well on light-color fabrics, but marks may be difficult to remove. White pencils work well on dark-color fabrics, and silver pencils show up well on many colors. Since chalk rubs off easily, it's a good choice if you are marking as you quilt. Fabric marking pens make more durable and visible markings, but the marks should be carefully removed according to manufacturer's instructions. Press down only as hard as necessary to make a visible line.

When you choose to mark your quilt, whether before or after the layers are basted together, is also a factor in deciding which marking tool to use. If you mark with chalk or a chalk pencil, handling the quilt during basting may rub off the markings. Intricate or ornamental designs may not be practical to mark as you quilt; mark these designs before basting using a more durable marker.

To choose marking tools, take all these factors into consideration and test different markers on scrap fabric until you find the one that gives the desired result.

Using Quilting Stencils

A wide variety of precut quilting stencils, as well as entire books of quilting patterns, are available. Using a stencil makes it easier to mark intricate or repetitive designs on your quilt top.

1. To make a stencil from a pattern, center template plastic over pattern and use a permanent marker to trace pattern onto plastic.

2. Use a craft knife with a single or double blade to cut narrow slits along traced lines (**Fig. 23**).

Fig. 23

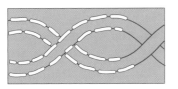

3. Use desired marking tool and stencil to mark quilting lines.

Choosing and Preparing the Backing

To allow for slight shifting of the quilt top during quilting, the backing should be approximately 4" larger on all sides for a bed-size quilt top or approximately 2" larger on all sides for a wall hanging. Yardage requirements listed for quilt backings are calculated for 45"w fabric. If you are making a bed-size quilt, using 90"w or 108"w fabric for the backing may eliminate piecing. To piece a backing using 45"w fabric, use the following instructions.

1. Measure length and width of quilt top; add 8" (4" for a wall hanging) to each measurement.
2. If quilt top is 76"w or less, cut backing fabric into 2 lengths slightly longer than the determined length measurement. Trim selvages. Place lengths with right sides facing and sew long edges together, forming a tube (**Fig. 24**). Match seams and press along 1 fold (**Fig. 25**). Cut along pressed fold to form a single piece (**Fig. 26**).

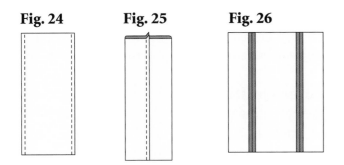

Fig. 24   **Fig. 25**   **Fig. 26**

3. If quilt top is more than 76"w, cut backing fabric into 3 lengths slightly longer than the determined width measurement. Trim selvages. Sew long edges together to form a single piece.
4. Trim backing to correct size, if necessary, and press seam allowances open.

Choosing and Preparing the Batting

Choosing the right batting will make your quilting job easier. For fine hand quilting, choose a low-loft batting in any of the fiber types described here. Machine quilters will want to choose a low-loft batting that is all cotton or a cotton/polyester blend because the cotton helps "grip" the layers of the quilt. If the quilt is to be tied, a high-loft batting, sometimes called extra-loft or fat batting, is a good choice.

Batting is available in many different fibers. Bonded polyester batting is one of the most popular batting types. It is treated with a protective coating to stabilize the fibers and to reduce "bearding," a process in which batting fibers work their way out through the quilt fabrics. Other batting options include cotton/polyester batting, which combines the best of both polyester and cotton battings; all-cotton batting, which must be quilted more closely than polyester batting; and wool and silk battings, which are generally more expensive and usually only dry-cleanable.

Whichever batting you choose, read the manufacturer's instructions closely for any special notes on care or preparation. When you're ready to use your chosen batting in a project, cut batting the same size as the prepared backing.

Assembling the Quilt

1. Examine wrong side of quilt top closely; trim any seam allowances and clip any threads that may show through the front of the quilt. Press quilt top.
2. If quilt top is to be marked before layering, mark quilting lines (see **Marking Quilting Lines**, page 106).
3. Place backing **wrong** side up on a flat surface. Use masking tape to tape edges of backing to surface. Place batting on top of backing fabric. Smooth batting gently, being careful not to stretch or tear. Center quilt top right side up on batting.
4. If hand quilting, begin in the center and work toward the outer edges to hand baste all layers together. Use long stitches and place basting lines approximately 4" apart (**Fig. 27**). Smooth fullness or wrinkles toward outer edges.

Fig. 27

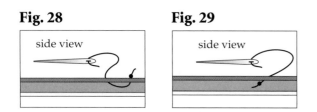

5. If machine quilting, use 1" rustproof safety pins to "pin-baste" all layers together, spacing pins approximately 4" apart. Begin at the center and work toward the outer edges to secure all layers. If possible, place pins away from areas that will be quilted, although pins may be removed as needed when quilting.

Hand Quilting

The quilting stitch is a basic running stitch that forms a broken line on the quilt top and backing. Stitches on the quilt top and backing should be straight and equal in length.

1. Secure center of quilt in hoop or frame. Check quilt top and backing to make sure they are smooth. To help prevent puckers, always begin quilting in the center of the quilt and work toward the outside edges.

2. Thread needle with an 18"-20" length of quilting thread; knot 1 end. Using a thimble, insert needle into quilt top and batting approximately 1/2" from where you wish to begin quilting. Bring needle up at the point where you wish to begin (**Fig. 28**); when knot catches on quilt top, give thread a quick, short pull to "pop" knot through fabric into batting (**Fig. 29**).

Fig. 28   **Fig. 29**

side view	side view

3. Holding the needle with your sewing hand and placing your other hand underneath the quilt, use thimble to push the tip of the needle down through all layers. As soon as needle touches your finger underneath, use that finger to push the tip of the needle only back up through the layers to top of quilt. (The amount of the needle showing above the fabric determines the length of the quilting stitch.) Referring to **Fig. 30**, rock the needle up and down, taking 3 - 6 stitches before bringing the needle and thread completely through the layers. Check the back of the quilt to make sure stitches are going through all layers. When quilting through a seam allowance or quilting a curve or corner, you may need to make 1 stitch at a time.

Fig. 30

4. When you reach the end of your thread, knot thread close to the fabric and "pop" knot into batting; clip thread close to fabric.

5. Stop and move your hoop as often as necessary. You do not have to tie a knot every time you move your hoop; you may leave the thread dangling and pick it up again when you return to that part of the quilt.

Machine Quilting

The following instructions are for straight-line quilting, which requires a walking foot or even-feed foot. The term "straight-line" is somewhat deceptive, since curves (especially gentle ones) as well as straight lines can be stitched with this technique.

1. Wind your sewing machine bobbin with general-purpose thread that matches the quilt backing. Do not use quilting thread. Thread the needle of your machine with transparent monofilament thread if you want your quilting to blend with your quilt top fabrics. Use decorative thread, such as a metallic or contrasting-color general-purpose thread, when you want the quilting lines to stand out more. Set the stitch length for 6 - 10 stitches per inch and attach the walking foot to sewing machine.

2. After pin-basting, decide which section of the quilt will have the longest continuous quilting line, oftentimes the area from center top to center bottom. Leaving the area exposed where you will place your first line of quilting, roll up each edge of the quilt to help reduce the bulk, keeping fabrics smooth. Smaller projects may not need to be rolled.

3. Start stitching at beginning of longest quilting line, using very short stitches for the first ¼" to "lock" beginning of quilting line. Stitch across project, using one hand on each side of the walking foot to slightly spread the fabric and to guide the fabric through the machine. Lock stitches at end of quilting line.

4. Continue machine quilting, stitching longer quilting lines first to stabilize the quilt before moving on to other areas.

Machine Stipple Quilting

The term "stipple quilting" refers to dense quilting using a meandering line of machine stitching or closely spaced hand stitching.

1. Wind your sewing machine bobbin with general-purpose thread that matches the quilt backing. Do not use quilting thread. Thread the needle of your machine with transparent monofilament thread if you want your quilting to blend with your quilt top fabrics. Use decorative thread, such as a metallic or contrasting-colored general-purpose thread, when you want the quilting lines to stand out more.

2. For random stipple quilting, use a darning foot, drop or cover feed dogs, and set stitch length at zero. Pull up bobbin thread and hold both thread ends while you stitch 2 or 3 stitches in place to lock thread. Cut threads near quilt surface. Place hands lightly on quilt on either side of darning foot.

3. Begin stitching in a meandering pattern (**Fig. 31**), guiding the quilt with your hands. The object is to make stitches of similar length and to not sew over previous stitching lines. The movement of your hands is what determines the stitch length; it takes practice to coordinate your hand motions and the pressure you put on the foot pedal, so go slowly at first.

Fig. 31

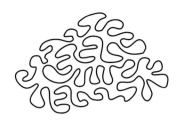

4. Continue machine quilting, filling in one open area of the quilt before moving on to another area, locking thread again at end of each line of stitching by sewing 2 or 3 stitches in place and trimming thread ends.

BINDING

Binding encloses the raw edges of your quilt. Because of its stretchiness, bias binding works well for binding projects with curves or rounded corners and tends to lie smooth and flat in any given circumstance. It is also more durable than other types of binding.

Making Continuous Bias Strip Binding

Bias strips for binding can simply be cut and pieced to the desired length. However, when a long length of binding is needed, the "continuous" method is quick and accurate.

1. Cut a square from binding fabric the size indicated in the project instructions. Cut square in half diagonally to make 2 triangles.

2. With right sides together and using a ¼" seam allowance, sew triangles together (**Fig. 32**); press seam allowance open.

Fig. 32

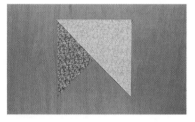

3. On wrong side of fabric, draw lines the width of the binding as specified in the project instructions, usually 2¹/₂" (**Fig. 33**). Cut off any remaining fabric less than this width.

Fig. 33

4. With right sides inside, bring short edges together to form a tube; match raw edges so that first drawn line of top section meets second drawn line of bottom section (**Fig. 34**).

Fig. 34

5. Carefully pin edges together by inserting pins through drawn lines at the point where drawn lines intersect, making sure the pins go through intersections on both sides. Using a ¹/₄" seam allowance, sew edges together. Press seam allowance open.
6. To cut continuous strip, begin cutting along first drawn line (**Fig. 35**). Continue cutting along drawn line around tube.

Fig. 35

7. Trim ends of bias strip square.
8. Matching wrong sides and raw edges, press bias strip in half lengthwise to complete binding.

Making Straight-Grain Binding

Binding may also be cut from the straight lengthwise or crosswise grain of the fabric. You will find that straight-grain binding works well for small projects and projects with straight edges.

1. Measure each edge of quilt; add 3" to each measurement. Cut lengthwise or crosswise strips of binding fabric the width called for in the project instructions. Strips may be pieced to achieve the necessary length.
2. Matching wrong sides and raw edges, press binding in half lengthwise.

Attaching Binding With Mitered Corners

1. Press 1 end of binding diagonally (**Fig. 36**).

Fig. 36

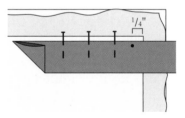

2. Beginning with pressed end several inches from a corner, lay binding around quilt to make sure that seams in binding will not end up at a corner. Adjust placement if necessary. Matching raw edges of binding to raw edge of quilt top, pin binding to right side of quilt along 1 edge.
3. When you reach the first corner, mark ¹/₄" from corner of quilt top (**Fig. 37**).

Fig. 37

4. Using a ¹/₄" seam allowance, sew binding to quilt, backstitching at beginning of stitching and when you reach the mark (**Fig. 38**). Lift needle out of fabric and clip thread.

Fig. 38

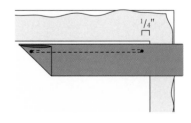

5. Fold binding as shown in **Figs. 39** and **40** and pin binding to adjacent side, matching raw edges. When you reach the next corner, mark $1/4$" from edge of quilt top.

Fig. 39   **Fig. 40**

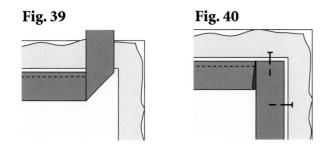

6. Backstitching at edge of quilt top, sew pinned binding to quilt (**Fig. 41**); backstitch when you reach the next mark. Lift needle out of fabric and clip thread.

Fig. 41

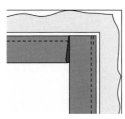

7. Repeat Steps 5 and 6 to continue sewing binding to quilt until binding overlaps beginning end by approximately 2". Trim excess binding.

8. If using $2^1/2$" w binding (finished size $1/2$"), trim backing and batting a scant $1/4$" larger than quilt top so that batting and backing will fill the binding when it is folded over to the quilt backing. If using narrower binding, trim backing and batting even with edges of quilt top.

9. On 1 edge of quilt, fold binding over to quilt backing and pin pressed edge in place, covering stitching line (**Fig. 42**). On adjacent side, fold binding over, forming a mitered corner (**Fig. 43**). Repeat to pin remainder of binding in place.

Fig. 42   **Fig. 43**

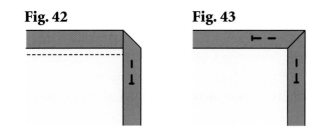

10. Blind stitch binding to backing, taking care not to stitch through to front of quilt.

Blind Stitch
Come up at 1. Go down at 2 and come up at 3. Length of stitches may be varied as desired (**Fig. 44**).

Fig. 44

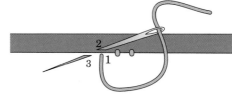

MAKING A HANGING SLEEVE
Attaching a hanging sleeve to the back of your wall hanging or quilt before the binding is added allows you to display your completed project on a wall.

1. Measure the width of the wall hanging top and subtract 1". Cut a piece of fabric 7"w by the determined measurement.
2. Press short edges of fabric piece $1/4$" to wrong side; press edges $1/4$" to wrong side again and machine stitch in place.
3. Matching wrong sides, fold piece in half lengthwise to form a tube.
4. Follow project instructions to sew binding to quilt top and to trim backing and batting. Before blind stitching binding to backing, match raw edges and stitch hanging sleeve to center top edge on back of wall hanging.
5. Finish binding wall hanging, treating the hanging sleeve as part of the backing.
6. Blind stitch bottom of hanging sleeve to backing, taking care not to stitch through to front of quilt.
7. Insert dowel or slat into hanging sleeve.

EMBROIDERY STITCH
Stem Stitch
Come up at 1. Keeping thread below the stitching line, go down at 2 and come up at 3. Go down at 4 and come up at 5 (**Fig. 45**).

Fig. 45

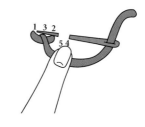

SIGNING AND DATING YOUR QUILT

Your completed quilt is a work of art and should be signed and dated. There are many different ways to do this, and you should pick a method that reflects the style of the quilt, the occasion for which it was made, and your own particular talents.

The following suggestions may give you an idea for recording the history of your quilt for future generations.

• Embroider your name, the date, and any additional information on the quilt top or backing. You may choose embroidery floss colors that closely match the fabric you are working on, such as white floss on a white border, or contrasting colors may be used.

• Make a label from muslin and use a permanent marker to write your information. Your label may be as plain or as fancy as you wish. Stitch the label to the back of the quilt.

• Chart a cross-stitch label design that includes the information you wish and stitch it in colors that complement the quilt. Stitch the finished label to the quilt backing.

Metric Conversion Chart

Inches x 2.54 = centimeters (cm)	Yards x .9144 = meters (m)	
Inches x 25.4 = millimeters (mm)	Yards x 91.44 = centimeters (cm)	
Inches x .0254 = meters (m)	Centimeters x .3937 = inches (")	
	Meters x 1.0936 = yards (yd)	

Standard Equivalents

1/8"	3.2 mm	0.32 cm	1/8 yard	11.43 cm	0.11 m
1/4"	6.35 mm	0.635 cm	1/4 yard	22.86 cm	0.23 m
3/8"	9.5 mm	0.95 cm	3/8 yard	34.29 cm	0.34 m
1/2"	12.7 mm	1.27 cm	1/2 yard	45.72 cm	0.46 m
5/8"	15.9 mm	1.59 cm	5/8 yard	57.15 cm	0.57 m
3/4"	19.1 mm	1.91 cm	3/4 yard	68.58 cm	0.69 m
7/8"	22.2 mm	2.22 cm	7/8 yard	80 cm	0.8 m
1"	25.4 mm	2.54 cm	1 yard	91.44 cm	0.91 m

We have made every effort to ensure that these instructions are accurate and complete. We cannot, however, be responsible for human error, typographical mistakes, or variations in individual work.

Production Team: Technical Writer – Andrea Ahlen; Editorial Writer – Susan McManus Johnson; Lead Graphic Artist- Jenny Dickerson; Graphic Artist- Chad Brown